GULF COAST
OYSTERS

GULF COAST OYSTERS

CLASSIC & MODERN RECIPES *of a* SOUTHERN RENAISSANCE

IRV MILLER

SPRING HOUSE PRESS

52

112

202

172

CONTENTS

GULF OYSTERS, REVISITED

A Foreword from Bill Walton, Dr. Oyster

There was a time when I didn't know better; when I thought that all oysters from the Gulf of Mexico were muddy, huge, and bland. Living and working in New England, I thought this was true, though I hadn't tried all that many oysters from the Gulf. It didn't help that during my visit to interview with Auburn University, my wife, Beth, and I stopped at a famous raw bar in Mobile, Alabama, ordered a dozen, and got . . . muddy, huge, bland oysters.

I got the job and celebrated months later at that same raw bar—and I was served some of the best oysters I had ever tasted. They were plump and firm, with dash of salt and the pure flavors of the local waters. That was the true beginning of my realization of what Gulf Coast oysters have been and could be.

The Gulf oyster industry has been built on the beds of oysters sprinkled in the protected, nutrient-rich coastal waters of the Gulf. Whether from private leases or public reefs, the oysters here rely on recruitment of wild oysters via spat fall that attaches to the cultch (i.e., shell or other hard substrate). This can allow for banner years, but can also mean down years from high levels of predation, dramatic salinity changes, and poor recruitment. Because these oysters form irregular shapes, they are primarily sent to the shucked market.

Now, at least in part because of a few down years, there's an effort to farm oysters. Off-bottom farming is the culture of oysters held in some type of basket, bag, or cage suspended or floating above the seafloor, with the intent of producing premium oysters for the half-shell market. Oysters grown this way are typically hatchery-reared, single-set oysters instead of the clumps of oysters found in the wild. This protects oysters from predators and getting buried in the mud. It also lets the farmer produce a world-class oyster over and over, with each farmer able to produce a distinct variety, much like microbrews or wines.

With new farms currently producing oysters in Alabama, Florida, and Louisiana (and Mississippi looking to get started), the growers and, thankfully, chefs have embraced this variety. Each farmer, working in the farm's natural environment, while making decisions about how to tend the crop, produces a distinct merroir—a term meaning "the flavor of the sea," though I'm now convinced the farmer affects how the oysters look and even taste, to some extent. This has created tremendous opportunity. Farmers can build their own brands and revive heritage oysters. Chefs and raw bars can offer menus with more than a dozen varieties produced in the Gulf. And, of course, oyster lovers can enjoy the fruits of these labors.

For me, it is about all that—and I've enjoyed more than my fair share of these amazing oysters on the half shell—but it's about more. It's about how we can rebuild rural coastal communities, provide good jobs, and keep traditions (or start new ones), all while protecting the environment and water quality.

It is with great pleasure that I welcome the passion and love that chef Irv Miller brings to the oyster renaissance in the Gulf of Mexico. This is a labor of love, and I believe it makes us more than we were.

THE OYSTER, EVOLVED

A Foreword from Jason Burnett, Oyster-Obsession.com

Not long ago in *A Geography of Oysters*, Rowan Jacobsen noted, "Gulf oysters are usually sold as generic oysters—indicative of a region that pays less attention to the nuances of different raw oysters than to their culinary possibilities." How quickly things change. Recently, at one of my favorite pubs in Birmingham, Alabama, I savored 10 different oysters, half of them farmed along the Gulf.

While the rise of off-bottom farming inspires a new appreciation of raw Gulf oysters, we also remain passionate about the culinary possibilities. At the same pub, they had oyster mac and cheese with orecchiette, smoked gouda, and white cheddar; baked oysters with bacon, blue cheese, and housemade hot sauce; fried oysters with sriracha aioli and jalapeño relish; an oyster roll with bacon, spinach, cream cheese, asparagus, jalapeño, cilantro, and sambal aioli; and oysters Rockefeller with absinthe foam. Cooks of all stripes approach oysters with the inventiveness applied to other seafood.

Cooked oysters are nothing new to North America, and certainly not unique to the Gulf. Native Americans roasted oysters. The earliest English settlers brought recipes for stewed, scalloped, and pickled oysters. Oyster bars dominated the pub scene from New York to San Francisco throughout the 19th century. But on the Gulf Coast, oyster cookery achieved glorification, and there's little arguing that New Orleans is the epicenter of cooked oysters. It is the home of oysters Rockefeller, Bienville, Roffignac, Lafitte, Mosca, Weemo, and countless other dishes that celebrate the bivalve.

While Louisiana's oyster culture is well documented by John Folse, Glenda and Jerald Horst, and others, Gulf Coast oyster tradition is by no means limited to the Bayou State. For more than a century, oyster harvesting, processing, and canning operations lined the coast from Texas to south Florida. Antique postcards document oyster fleets in Galveston and Palacios, Texas; Biloxi, Mississippi; Mobile, Alabama; and Apalachicola and St. Petersburg, Florida. With inexpensive oysters readily available year-round, it's no surprise that a culinary tradition developed around them.

Today, our obsession with oysters continues to stretch culinary creativity. Every November, as many as sixty chefs from across the region gather at Gulf Shores for the Hangout Oyster Cook-Off. Each chef creates a take on the Rockefeller, an original raw oyster topping, and a Cajun-style oyster (meats, cheeses, and spices encouraged). Eight thousand oyster lovers attend and are treated to scores of completely original and often extraordinary dishes.

Few people understand and appreciate the Gulf region's culinary history as well as author and chef Irv Miller. He not only recognized that the Gulf (especially the stretch known as the Redneck Riviera) has its own cuisine and culinary traditions beyond New Orleans, but his decades of work in some of the region's signature restaurants helped shape those traditions. His exploration of Gulf Coast oysters should prove to be both mouthwatering and enlightening to oyster lovers everywhere.

INTRODUCTION

Back in 1982, there was little to do in Destin, Florida—the World's Luckiest Fishing Village—except for day-boat fishing, hitting the beaches, making a trip to the local seafood market, or just stopping by the Jitney Jungle grocery store for supplies. That was the year I moved to the Gulf Coast. I vividly remember the liquor store's giant lime-green Green Knight, a statue holding a marquee, that stood majestically on Highway 98, a Destin landmark. The city had just installed new traffic lights and street signs, which stood out, yet the traffic volume throughout the seasons remained sparse. The traffic was especially light heading into sunset when the locals made their way to the bars and restaurants: the only social things to do. The best part was that Apalachicola oysters were abounding to the southeast, and fish from the Gulf of Mexico were plentiful.

In those days, instead of white tablecloths, restaurants used hardwood-resin tables covered with vinyl-checkerboard tablecloths, which were perfectly suitable for feasting on fried fish with hushpuppies or grabbing a seat at the oyster bar. Caroline Stuart, friend and author of *The Florida Cookbook,* paraphrased Panhandle culture as a recipe: "Equal parts rich resources and creative cooks, a Dash of Cracker ingenuity, a pinch of sophistication mixed with good ole' boy modesty, and served with low-key hospitality." Change happened slowly along this stretch of the Gulf Coast, and little had changed during that decade. As I settled in, I quickly learned that it was going to be a challenge for me to get local support for the highfalutin' food that I was trained for, so, it was back to the basics for me.

The home-spun restaurant food from that period was predictable and somewhat unfashionable, with none of today's 21st century menu malarkey. What you ordered is what you got. None of the chefs in town had culinary degrees, and that was fine with the locals. The culture there was slow-moving and the locals liked it that way. I had spent a good number of years living the simple life along the mid-Atlantic Coast, so when I discovered the quaint Destin village, I fell in love with its seemingly uncharted style.

However, at 28 years old, I was still the new kid in town, so I had to learn how to adapt and earn my acceptance into the local community. My plan was twofold: to win over the locals and appeal to the tastes of seasonal tourists from Alabama, Louisiana, Tennessee, Georgia, and Texas. This is where my training and knowledge from the Culinary Institute and subsequent time spent in San Antonio kicked in. So, I gave the people what they really wanted all along: New Orleans favorites such as Oysters Rockefeller and Oysters Bienville, in a quaint French restaurant called Les Saisons. It was here that I began experimenting with menu items such as cooked Gulf "Oysters du Jour." Nobody was whisking up beurre blanc (white butter sauce) or any fancy French sauces in that area at the time, nor was any kitchen using a chinois (fine strainer for sauces). Now was the moment for me to put into practice what I had learned the last few years at the CIA and the training I had received under a French chef in Texas.

The moment that I had a strong understanding of the local home-style foods of this Gulf Coast micro-region, endeared by many as the Redneck Riviera, I put my heart into creating new oyster toppings akin to the region, but used flavors no one had tasted before. My main source for oysters was Apalachicola Bay, just 160 miles away to the southeast. Apalachicola oysters (*Crassostrea virginica*) were delivered to us by the sack; after they made the two-and-a-half-hour journey up Highway 98, we shucked them for topping and baking.

I wasn't serving raw oysters on the half shell at Les Saisons during those early days. Most raw oysters were being served at the local hole-in-the-wall oyster bars, harbor-side beach shacks, and the bigger tourist-oriented seafood restaurants. By the late 1980s, raw bars came into vogue at some of the white tablecloth hot spots like Bud and Alley's in Seaside, Florida, where I was chef through the late '80s and early '90s. The bartenders, much to their surprise, soon found themselves doubling as oyster shuckers. All the while, my penchant for cooking oysters with toppings remained the same.

ABILITY WITH AVAILABILITY

As early as the mid-1800s, oyster beds in the Northwest's Pacific waters had mostly been decimated, with some just barely holding on into the following century. At around the same time on the Northeast and mid-Atlantic coastlines, oyster beds also began to empty. The collapse of fisheries along the Atlantic coast caused an explosion in oystering along the Gulf of Mexico. Even through the year 2000, the Gulf states produced most of the Eastern oysters for the country's limitlessly healthy appetite. Apalachicola, the most renowned location for its

Oyster shell pile at Buddy Ward and Sons Seafood on 13 Mile Road along Apalachicola Bay for rebuilding reefs and creating substrate.

namesake oysters, experienced a serious decline in their harvest by the mid-1980s, but seafood wholesalers were still able to provide a steady supply.

Following their long drought of ample oyster supplies, European oyster farmers brought their expertise to California and Washington. Here is where they pioneered oyster basket farming, and the Northeast followed suit throughout the 1970s and early '80s. By the 1990s, several folks along the Gulf of Mexico made attempts at farming oysters merely for experimental reasons, but were then commercially successful a decade later. Farmed oysters began to grow effectively in Alabama with the expertise of northern Cape Cod transplants and the aquaculture expertise of Bill Walton (no, not the NBA player). Now, oysters are being raised and harvested from much of the Gulf waters.

The famous Gulf oyster (a general name given to wild oysters harvested from various Gulf Coast bays and beds) was the workhorse of the Gulf, and way of life for oyster fishermen stretching from east of Florida's big bend to the coast of Texas was in trouble. Accustomed to climate variations and trials, the great Gulf waters remained insuperable, healthy, and production abundant, while continuing to supply most of the country's wild oysters. As production remained heavy, so did the prospects of continuing challenges for these Gulf Coast oysters. The threats— oyster drill, vibrio bacteria threat, drought and lack of fresh water flow, a series of hurricanes, and the 2010 Deepwater Horizon disaster were all game changers for Gulf fisheries. Oyster production along the Gulf states was in distress. Misfortune was looming for the Gulf oyster.

HOME IS WHERE THE OYSTER IS

There are five Gulf Coast oyster–producing states: Alabama, Florida, Mississippi, Louisiana, and Texas. Gulf Coast oysters, often considered a commodity oyster, are identified by the state or area from which they were harvested.

The majority of wild-harvested oysters is intended for the shucked market, both raw and cooked, rather than the premium half-shell market. Gulf Coast oysters are considered for slurping raw, but are most often used in cooked-topping creations. They vary in size from 3 to 4 inches, and often larger. To harvest these unmanicured clustered oysters, tongs and rake machines (i.e., dredge) scrape the bottom of the bay.

We're growing a new oyster from seed and above the seafloor... producing uniquely different-tasting succulent gems.

Once the harvest reaches the boat, oystermen use a hammer to cull them, discard the mud-filled ones, then rinse and clean the good ones. The larger oysters are sometimes mild-flavored, and create the perfect canvas for a broad range of flavor enhancements: fried, poached, grilled, roasted, or baked. Generations of Gulf Coast seafood fanatics, like my good friend and oyster authority Jim Gossen from Texas, prefer the big-bellied, briny, and supple oyster raw or cooked!

For better or worse, times are changing along the Gulf Coast. Now, folks who travel frequently and love raw oysters slurp a variety of the region's

INTRODUCTION

tastiest farmed oysters at upscale restaurant raw bars and oyster bars all around the country. They know it's common practice at restaurants for farmed oysters to be bought by the piece (singles), yet this concept is rarely seen at Gulf Coast restaurants. But here's the game changer: now we're growing a new oyster from seed and above the seafloor, and there are dozens of oyster farms producing uniquely different-tasting succulent gems in several Gulf states.

The familiar and affordable wild Gulf Coast oysters bought by the pound, provided by the sack, and sold by the dozen at local restaurants and oyster bars, are now experiencing a big cultural shift. Off-bottom oyster farmers who buy the oyster seed from a hatchery can grow them to market size in about as little as 10 months, and simply look to get a better return for their investment. Often, oyster seeds the size of a pin head are less expensive to the oyster rancher, but have a high mortality rate. Dime-sized oyster seeds are more expensive, but have a lower mortality rate. Other ranchers have invested in the hatchery equipment to cultivate their own larval seedlings and can offer them for less. Nevertheless, there's a new oyster in town—the off-bottom farm-raised oyster. A pristine farm-raised oyster can rival some of the tastiest cold water, farm-produced oysters in the country.

An unfortunate by-product from the decline of the wild oyster and their natural sets is that Gulf Coast oysters are no longer quite so cheap. Here in the Gulf states, raw bars still sell wild oysters by the dozen and half-dozen, and compared to anywhere else, they are still affordable. Here's the trick though: when people pay more for wild oysters, oyster farmers can afford to grow them right. As Rowan Jacobsen put it, "when you give a Gulf oyster space, salty water, and an occasional shake to keep it from growing too fast, you get an oyster that's the envy of the world." But the days of knocking back a dozen wild Gulf oysters for 12 bucks is slipping away forever. Right now, a dozen farmed oysters in NYC or New Orleans will cost you 38 dollars!

And while the overall cost of doing business has increased to meet the demands of the consumer, there's been a steady harvest decline not only for wild oysters themselves, but the oystering folks who live off the bay. Wild oysters are becoming increasingly expensive to sustainably harvest. Regulation changes, such as strict bay closures to protect the species, can force a fisherman to relocate. By and large, this is the reason interest in alternative oyster growing began along the Gulf Coast. Jobs are now being created and the future remains hopeful for oyster farming. I fully embrace the farm-raised oyster—it's the oyster of the future. The off-bottom farmed oyster could help sustain the wild oyster natural sets throughout the Gulf regions.

The off-bottom farmed oyster could help sustain the wild oyster natural sets throughout the Gulf regions.

21ST CENTURY BACK-BAY FARMING

Bill Walton (Auburn University Associate Professor) and Alabama entrepreneur Steve Crockett were the first to successfully pioneer oyster farming along

Oyster ranches in Oyster Bay in Panacea, Florida, are partnering with Wakulla Environmental Institute (WEI).

Alabama's bay back in 2009. They have both learned from mistakes and survived the unforeseen. Pristine water quality is not always a guarantee, and the Gulf of Mexico's bay waters are often at risk. Inclement weather conditions, too much or not enough rain, red tide, and the struggles inherited from oyster fishermen are an annual challenge for hard-working, serious oyster farmers. Since 2009, there have been a growing number of outfits along the Gulf carving out a niche for small-batch, premium, Southern-raised oysters. These are some of the prettiest, tastiest, deepest-cupped oysters in the marketplace.

Along the Gulf of Mexico, the oyster culture varies from state to state, as does the taste of an oyster from place to place; just ask any oyster purist. Nevertheless, it's hard to convince both the Gulf Coast oyster consumer and Gulf Coast industry folks of this cultural-shift struggle that is being experienced within the oyster industry in this region. It's about accepting premium farm-raised oysters and getting them onto menus, yet identifying oysters by their heritage bay.

In this book, I plan to share my oyster-culture discoveries with you as I visit oyster farms across the Gulf of Mexico. Someone had to do an oyster memoir to include the Redneck Riviera, I just happened to think of it first. Things usually happen a little slower along the Florida Panhandle and our neighbors to the west, and I like it that way. The casual lifestyle of the Gulf Coast lends itself to ample outdoor entertaining and gatherings: barbecues, shrimp and crab boils, fish fries, oyster roasts, or just raw oyster shucking from the back of a pickup truck. I love this place!

Please thumb through this cookbook and celebrate the sensible and delicious raw oyster sauces, as well as the topping recipes for premium farm-raised Gulf Coast oysters, and savor the Gulf Coast traditional cooked-oyster culture for large Gulf Coast oysters from the country's last great bays.

CHAPTER 1

THE ICONIC & INSURMOUNTABLE GULF COAST OYSTER

DIVING IN

The Gulf of Mexico is known as the American "Fertile Crescent" of seafood, particularly when it comes to oysters. Rowan Jacobsen, in his book *A Geography of Oysters,* says, "European explorers were amazed by early accounts of the region which claimed that oysters grew on trees." Metaphorically speaking, this statement makes sense because oysters were so abundant at the time—though oysters have been observed growing on mangrove tree roots, pilings, poles, and ropes in many Gulf tidal zones since then. Jacobsen also claims that *Crassostrea virginica,* the Gulf oyster, does "not have the strongest taste of any oyster, but does have the cleanest. It tastes of the sea and not much else, and for that reason it should be the oyster against which all others should be measured."

The Eastern oyster (*C. virginica*) is native from the northern reaches of Prince Edward Island down through Cape Cod and the Chesapeake; on to Apalachicola, New Orleans, and Texas; and then south through the Caribbean and the Yucatan Peninsula. Oyster reefs on the West Coast have the exotic Pacific or Japanese oyster, *C. gigas,* and the native Olympia oyster, *Ostreola conchaphila,* which can even be found in California and Washington.

The oyster reefs of the northern Gulf of Mexico are noteworthy on a national scale, largely because they are still there. The temperate waters of the Gulf provide exceptional environmental conditions for the Eastern oysters, making them abundant, fast growing, delicious, large, and affordable. The industry, which stretches from Florida to Texas, produces more wild oysters than any other region in the country, and most come from Louisiana's ample reefs.

FOOD AND GROWTH

Generally, Gulf Coast oysters grow subtidally, below mean low tide. Oysters grow along most Gulf Coast bays, as well as the East Coast saltwater creeks, riverbanks, and exposed mud flats. In shallower waters, these oysters can experience rapidly changing temperatures, including freezing air during the winter, but are rarely killed by extremes of temperature. However, oyster productivity varies within each bay system. The amount of food in the water and the water's temperature can affect whether the meat will be lean or plump, and how much the oyster grows.

When water temperatures increase into the 64 to 68°F range, oysters will spawn (i.e., release eggs and sperm). This process generally begins in May and continues somewhat into September. Once the eggs have been fertilized, in as little as 24 hours they hatch into free-swimming larvae. These miniature and immature beings have very limited motion, mostly moving with the tides and the currents. Two to three weeks after hatching, they settle to the bottom, where they must locate a hard, clean surface for permanent attachment. Larvae that are unable to find a suitable place for attachment will sink to the bottom and die! Larvae secrete a fluid that permanently adheres the left shell to the surface of attachment, and the newly attached oysters—called spat—never move again. It appears that almost any hard, clean surface is acceptable, but other oyster shells seem to be the most-favored surface. Oyster shells that are purposefully planted to attract oyster larvae are known as "cultch."

Gulf Coast oysters grow rapidly, at a rate of about 2 to 3 inches in as little as 10 to 12 months, whereas in colder, northern waters, that growth can take 2 to 4 years. Growth rates can be affected by temperature, food quantity, salinity, and disease. Shell growth usually occurs in the spring, and soft-body tissue growth occurs after spawning. Many Gulf oysters are so large because bottom-raised wild oysters harvested in the Gulf states—Florida, Alabama, Mississippi, Louisiana, and Texas—must reach the minimal legal market size of 3 inches. This enables the oysters to continue to grow even larger in the wild.

SUSTAINABILITY AND SURVIVABILITY

As members of the bivalve-mollusks group, both oysters and clams live in marine or brackish habitats. As filter-feeders, they consume free-swimming algae by filtering their food from the water, thus improving water quality. They open their shells to filter food from the water and close their shells for protection from predators and to prevent drying out. As generations of oysters settle on top of each other and grow, they form natural reefs that provide structured habitat for many fish and crab species.

The shallow, pristine Apalachicola Bay was once known for its abundant namesake oysters. The decline of oyster production there has

been caused by natural occurrences including hurricanes, drought, flooding, oyster-drill parasite, mud worms, boring sponge, and red tide. Recent droughts in the Southeast caused the freshwater flow from northern Georgia to Apalachicola Bay to be curtailed significantly. In addition, Florida also lost an ongoing battle to cap Georgia's water use, asserting that Peach State farmers and cities were using too much water, causing low river flows in the Florida Panhandle. The lack of flow from the north resulted in an unhealthy imbalance in the estuaries. Basically, more seawater was getting in than freshwater. It can be said that those causes are indirectly related to human interference with nature, but the Deepwater Horizon oil spill in 2010 was a direct consequence. Ironically, the event triggered a panic to over-harvest the oysters in Apalachicola, even though the oil never reached the bay.

Similar circumstances affect oyster reefs and production for all five states along the Gulf of Mexico. It's nearly impossible to recover fully after battling all the circumstances that have occurred over the many decades, which is why aquaculture has become even more important in the sustainability of the wild Gulf Coast oyster. Aquaculture has now become an official, viable option for state legislators to consider. The Gulf Coast oyster has had a long, prolific history, and in its natural set has seen its period of decline, but is now making its comeback using alternative oyster growing methods.

MERROIR:
The Terroir of the Sea

In the 21st century, oysters have often been described by the same elevated prose usually associated with wines. The term merroir is a word coined back in 2003 by *Seattle Times* writer Jon Rowley and his friend, Chef Greg Atkinson, that simply means the group of characteristics oysters acquire from their natural environment and the water in which they live. In the world of wine, the grape tells you the whole story—the appellation and its climate, the vineyard and its soil, and the vintner's technique for making the wine. For the American oyster, this boils down to the bay's influence. The story is told by the bay or estuary, distinct climate influences, and the grower's method of care and cultivation. Essentially, merroir is underwater terroir. The oyster's unique physical characteristics begin with size, cup, shape, and degree of clarity. Flavor nuances can vary from mild to sharp brininess and full body, with some "kelpier" than others, while yet others are sweet, creamy, and buttery, with a clean, crisp finish. Again, these descriptions may strike you as easily attributable to the nuances of white wines.

I am a ostreaphile of both wild bottom-cultivated and off-bottom cultivated farm-raised oysters. Off-bottom farmed oysters are certain to be the Gulf Coast's great oyster comeback, yet there are still hundreds of varieties of wild oysters growing in natural and rebuilt reef sets along the Gulf Coast from Louisiana to Florida. They are all still from the same species of Eastern oyster (*C. virginica*) and vary from state to state, but even oysters from the same bay can vary in size, salinity, meat content, and taste.

Understanding merroir is essential if you want to know how the oysters you're ordering will taste and feel in your mouth. It is the taste of the freshly shucked oyster, along with its liquor, slurped straight out of its shell that dictates the unique flavor nuances of the oyster in its purest form. Oyster purists believe that the geography and specifically where the oyster is grown are what makes the notable difference detected in its flavor.

How exactly does each oyster get its own unique flavor? Unsurprisingly, it's Mother Nature that provides the balancing act of salinity. Freshwater feeds the oysters' growing spot and interacts with the Gulf's salty, tidal action, often influenced by protective barrier islands, which contributes to survival, size, health, and flavor. However, remember that not only does the flavor depend on the type of oyster, water temperature, and where they are farmed, but also on the oyster's supply of phytoplankton, microscopic organisms, and general mineralogy generated by the seafloor. All of these factors come together to give the Gulf Coast oyster its exceptional flavor.

Camanada Bay sunset with shrimp boat; Grand Isle, Louisiana.

OFF-BOTTOM OYSTER FARMING
for the Gulf Coast

Murder Point oyster farmers harvesting oysters for a tasting.

Aquaculture and Fisheries Specialist Bill Walton and entrepreneur Steve Crockett of Point aux Pins Oyster Farm on Grand Bay in Bayou La Batre began experimenting with different types of off-bottom growing methods on Steve's 1-acre Alabama oyster farm business more than 7 years ago. "Off-bottom" means that the oysters never touch the sandy or sometimes muddy seafloor. This type of oyster aquaculture (mariculture) holds oysters in a mesh basket, bag, or cage that is kept above the bottom. This protects them from predators and from being buried below the muddied sand.

In the Gulf of Mexico, warmer waters let oysters reach market size in under 12 months, whereas it might take 2 to 4 years in other bays and inlets around the country's coastlines. Oyster farming also serves a dual function by being both naturally sustainable and environmentally friendly. Farmed oysters feed off the microscopic algae in the water, filtering up to 50 gallons of water each day through their gills to capture the nutrients. The water becomes cleaner and other sea life flourishes as a result, which ultimately is great for us.

GROW-OUT SYSTEMS FOR THE GULF COAST OYSTER

Gulf Coast oyster farmers are always finding new ways to raise oysters, but there are currently three common grow-out systems being used in the Gulf of Mexico. Each system allows oyster farmers the flexibility to make decisions about how to manage their crops based on their state's bay lease location and their respective tide pools.

The most basic kind are off-bottom cages with baskets. These sit on short platforms made of sturdy materials, such as PVC piping or wire cage materials, keeping the oysters just above the seafloor. Oyster farmers retrieve these by pulling the cages up to the surface either by hand, a pole and hook, or from a line attached to a float.

Another widely used system uses floating cages or baskets that float just below the surface. This technique allows the oysters to feed and grow while being flipped-over periodically by hand or boat, depending on the water depth and tide. When the baskets (or cages) are out of the water, both the oysters and their containers have a chance to dry out (desiccate) and get clean. More importantly, the quicker lift to the surface controls the fouling created by barnacles and secondary spat.

The other system uses adjustable Australian longlines, where baskets are strung along lines

Bill Walton sampling and sizing first harvest oysters for Pensacola Bay Oyster Co.

between pilings or PVC pipes. Along the line, there are pipes with tide clips that let the farmers decide at what tidal height they want to raise their oysters. Some farmers using this system will attach thick lengths of sturdy foam to each basket and remove the clips completely to let them rise and fall naturally with the tides.

Oyster farming may well complement the wild-harvest oyster fishery, given that a significant portion of wild-harvested oyster meat is intended for the shucked market, both raw and cooked, rather than

Oyster cages at Massacre Island, Alabama.

the premium singles market. Around the country, a premium farmed oyster is often ready for harvesting at 2 to 2 ½ inches. During my oyster farm outings (see page 32), I found that Florida, Louisiana, and Texas oyster farmers let them grow in their natural sets to 3 to 4 inches. Furthermore, in Gulf states, 3 inches is the minimum legal size for harvesting bottomland oysters.

I asked Bill Walton, "Why is it okay for an oyster farmer to produce a smaller oyster, when the legal size for wild oysters in Gulf states is 3 inches?" Bill replied, "the rationale is that a fishery needs oysters to be large enough to reproduce before they are harvested. Farmed oysters aren't expected to 'contribute' to the fishery, and are harvested off private farms, so they can be whatever size the market wants."

A 2- to 2 ½-inch Gulf Coast off-bottom raised oyster is considered ideally sized for the boutique or premium oyster market. A very competitive market has developed for these chic "high-born bivalves" up the Atlantic seaboard to the Northeast, and out to the West Coast and Pacific Northwest.

IDENTIFYING FARMED
Gulf Coast Oysters

COMMODITY VS. PREMIUM

People want to know where their seafood comes from, especially the origin of their Gulf Coast oysters. In the late 1800s, wild oysters adopted the name of the exact location they came from, but are often identified by their state of origin. Texas oyster expert Robb Walsh said it best: "At the time of the Civil War, oysters from Pepper Grove Reef in East Galveston Bay were very popular in oyster bars. So were the oysters from Lady's Pass and several other spots. Galveston Bay oysters were always identified by place name back in the late 1800s."

Somewhere along the way, the practice of collecting hundreds of sacks of oysters and then transporting them in one mass became second nature to the dealer. When you have a trailer-truck brimming with wild oysters, you might have three hundred sacks picked from three or four different fishermen, and they're all being sold as one lot. Therefore, they are processed and tagged to include the wholesaler's identification number, date of harvest, harvest area, name or number, type of shellfish, quantity of shellfish, a sell-by date, and are usually called by their accrual name such as Louisiana Oysters, Texas Oysters, Alabama Oysters, or simply Gulf Oysters.

The wild Gulf oyster still maintains this traditional method of collecting, sorting, and bulk-dealing from several small oyster boats throughout a region. To this day, bottom-harvested oysters are delivered as a representative of one state's oyster.

Conveyor at Bon Secour Fisheries used for sorting and culling Louisiana sack wild oysters.

That is what makes a commodity oyster. The commodity oyster is what the Gulf of Mexico has been famous for. But now an oyster origin revival along the Gulf Coast is underway for the bottom reef and particularly off-bottom cage-grown varieties.

MINDSET AND MARKET

The Gulf Coast off-bottom oyster farmer has now entered the premium oyster market; to market this 2 1/4- to 3-inch bivalve, purists prefer labeling with appellations. Farmed oysters taste different in each

OYSTER RECIPE SCORE		OYSTER	
BATTLE CREEK OYSTER — MID ATLANTIC	87	MOON SHOAL OYSTER — NEW ENGLAND	80
BLUE POOL OYSTER — PACIFIC NORTHWEST	82	MOONSTONE OYSTER — NEW ENGLAND	84
CAPERS BLADE OYSTER — MID ATLANTIC	75	MURDER POINT OYSTER — GULF	94
CHAMPAGNE BAY OYSTER — GULF	88	PEMAQUID OYSTER — NEW ENGLAND	83
EAST BEACH BLONDES — NEW ENGLAND	80	POINT AUX PINS — GULF	91
FAT BASTARD — PACIFIC NORTHWEST	85	QUONNIE ROCK — NEW ENGLAND	73
HAMA HAMA — PACIFIC NORTHWEST	79	SALT POND OYSTER — NEW ENGLAND	72
HOG ISLAND SWEETWATERS — CALIFORNIA	84	SEWANSECOTT — MID-ATLANTIC	79
ISLAND CREEK OYSTER — NEW ENGLAND	72	SHIGOKU — PACIFIC NORTHWEST	87
KUMAMOTO — PACIFIC NORTHWEST	90	STANDISH SHORE SELECTS — NEW ENGLAND	82
MATUNUCK OYSTER — NEW ENGLAND	80	TOTTEN INLET PACIFICS — PACIFIC NORTHWEST	86
		CHERRYSTONE — VIRGINIA	76

Half-shell oyster tasting scoreboard at the North American Oyster Showcase, Hangout Oyster Cook-Off in Gulf Shores, Alabama.

bay, and knowing the appellation for bottom-reef varieties allows the detection of taste differences versus off-bottom oysters from bay to bay. The oyster's name, place of origin, grower, and its typical characteristics are also important to the purist.

However, not all regions have this mindset. Many Florida oyster farmers are not as concerned with claiming fame to individual merroir, while some Alabama farmers located side-by-side in Sandy Bay feel strongly that their oysters both look and taste different because of the way they are nurtured. In Florida, Panacea Co-op members and student ranches are in the very same body of water in Wakulla County's Oyster Bay. Many are side-by-side, just an oyster toss away, sharing the St. Marks River and the percolating spring waters in their estuary. These individually farmed oysters are purchased through the co-op, and are represented as Panacea Pearls.

Some independent ranchers in Panacea's Oyster Bay and nearby Alligator Harbor brand their oysters with their company name, such as OysterMom Oysters and Saucey Lady Oysters. In Pensacola, Pensacola Bay Oyster Company names theirs for Escambia Bay's scenic highway locations and landmarks: Magnolia Bluff along the West Bay and Garcon Point along East Bay, both fed by different watersheds.

EVERY OYSTER HAS A STORY

Oyster-growing experiments began decades ago along both the Florida and Alabama Gulf Coast. Oyster grower's stories are as unique as the oysters themselves. My friend Bill Walton is unique for his experience and wealth of knowledge for not only attaining seed, but in supporting start-up oyster farmers and troubleshooting for off-bottom oyster growers throughout the Gulf states. Bill believes that the oyster-growing industry is still in its infancy along the coast of north Florida. Even decades-old Florida clam hatcheries have been experimenting with more oyster seeds during the past few years and they are still experimenting on how to effectively tend to their crops. The oyster seed supply is not quite enough to go around and the demand is high.

The grower, or rancher, dictates the nurturing of their floating cages, off-bottom cages, floating baskets, and longline baskets of oyster seeds and juveniles. They create their own unique, marketable oyster. The choice of growing method and technique alters the shell's shape and size, while incorporating the grower's individual philosophy and experience to hone their oysters for their target market. Some do little or nothing at all, which helps keep cost to a minimum and the oysters affordable. Off-bottom, cage-grown oysters set 6 inches off the bay bottom are a good example of a minimalist approach. Some are only handled 3 to 4 times during their growing cycle, mostly with infrequent sorting by tumbling. Quite often, the smaller ones are re-planted and not touched again until the farmer is ready to harvest.

Another factor is wet storage. This storage method uses filtered and recirculated seawater in tanks to temporarily hold oysters so they don't die before they arrive at their destination. This also helps to mediate supply interruptions due to rainfall closures. However, bundling different varieties in the same pool of water becomes controversial and often sounds dreadful to the oyster purist, affecting and distracting from the oyster's true flavor and natural salinity.

Ideally, identification measures for farmed oysters are something like this: visual-recognition, including its shape (length, width, and cup), size (inches), and markings (color, stripes, and typical biofouling); a parts per thousand (ppt) salinity test before open harvesting, indicating salt levels at a low (10) to high (30) number; and a blend of line items from state harvest/dealer tag details (see illustrations). This wealth of information allows the restaurants, raw bars, and public in general to identify their own favorite oyster.

─────── TYPICAL SIZING ───────
FOR OFF-BOTTOM
FARM-RAISED OYSTERS

Cocktail, Boutique, Premium: 2 to 3-inch

Selects: 3 to 4-inch

Large: 4 to 6-inch

This appears to be a promising start to the new, burgeoning coastal economy that could revitalize struggling fishing communities all along the Gulf states. Amid trying times for the wild oyster population in the Gulf states, there now appears to be a better way of identifying and acknowledging the emergent farmed oyster's birthright, and it is a top-quality product when compared to its natural counterpart. Restaurants, gastro-pubs, and oyster bars all around the country are cashing in on the growing detailed knowledge available on farmed oysters, including place of origin, availability, grower, price, handling, and preparation: the birth of the craft oyster.

Dealer tag.

PERISHABLE
KEEP
REFRIGERATED

NAME OF FIRM
MAILING ADDRESS OF FIRM
CITY, STATE & ZIP CODE
Phone #(---)-------

Wholesale # WD_____

Cert. # FL ####-SS, SO, RP, OR PHP'

ORIGINALS SHIPPERS CERT. NO. IF OTHER THAN ABOVE: _____
DATE OF HARVEST: _____
HARVEST AREA, NAME, OR #:_____
TYPE OF SHELLFISH: _____
QUANTITY OF SHELLFISH: _____
SELL BY: _____

THIS TAG IS REQUIRED TO BE ATTACHED UNTIL CONTAINER IS EMPTY
OR IS RETAGGED AND THEREAFTER KEPT ON FILE FOR 90 DAYS

EAT OYSTERS
WheneveR

One expression and unproven theory often heard in the oyster world is "Never eat oysters in a month without an R." Now let's see—May, June, July, and August—hey, those months don't have the letter R! In the Deep South, along the Gulf Coast, eating oysters all summer long is not unusual. After all, the word "summer" has an R in it, right? And what's in a letter, anyway?

Not to worry.

HISTORIC BACKGROUND

The Native Americans are alleged to have introduced this precaution centuries ago. The advice also dates back at least to 1599, when it appeared in Englishman Henry Buttes' cookbook, *Dyets Dry Dinner,* though some historians trace it to an obscure, ancient Latin saying.

FLAVOR

Storyteller and author M.F.K. Fisher grew up in Marseille and Dijon, France, and in 1941 published the iconic *Consider the Oyster.* People who have broken the rule and bought oysters in those forbidden months say —as Fisher put it—that they are "the most delicious then: full and flavorsome." She notes the discriminating rule is not stringent in Europe, and desirable taste is often of personal preference.

Texas author Robb Walsh, has determined that there's more science to the theory than one would expect, explaining, "the famous 'months without an R' saying came from Northern Europe, but the seasons are different for the Gulf of Mexico." In his book, *Sex, Death and Oysters,* Walsh explains:

Oyster meat becomes creamy before spat, which happens as the water begins to warm, then very thin, and translucent. This silky, sweet-cream texture is different from the oyster's texture the rest of the year. When water temperatures get colder at the end of the summer, oysters begin storing a carbohydrate compound called glycogen. To humans, glycogen tastes like sugar. As the water gets colder, more glycogen accumulates, and the oyster gets plumper and tastes sweeter. Gulf oysters are at their absolute peak at the coldest part of the winter. With the onset of warmer water temperatures in April, oysters begin to convert glycogen to gonad (reproductive material). As the summer approaches and temperature rises, the oyster progressively loses its sweetness, becoming more and more "fishy" tasting. It's not an unpleasant flavor—in fact many oyster lovers like it—but it isn't sweet.

I agree with Walsh.

This old dilemma has recently inspired a potential scientific fix by modifying oysters to avoid the processes that make them less tasty in the summer months. Here is a quick explanation.

There are two main types of oyster seeds being cultivated: diploid and triploid. A ploidy is the number of sets of chromosomes in a cell. Oysters found in nature are normally diploid, meaning they have two sets each of male and female

My first tasting of briny and supple full-sized Caminada Bay Oysters was here, at Dicky Brennan's Street Bourbon Bar in New Orleans.

chromosomes. Genetically manipulated triploids have two sets of female chromosomes and one set of male chromosomes.

Triploid oysters have two important advantages over diploid oysters during their life cycles. In the summer months, when regular diploid oysters are spawning (i.e., releasing eggs and sperm into the water, which makes the oyster meat lean and watery), they are often considered undesirable for slurping. Triploid oysters are reproductively sterile, so they are incapable of normal sexual maturation. This means triploid oysters remain firm, full, and sweet during the summer. This sterility also leads to improved growth rates, because they don't spend energy reproducing. Most farmers are experimenting and growing both types.

SPOILAGE

All around the country, specifically the Gulf of Mexico, oyster and shellfish production can be problematic during the summer. Historically, warm months made for bad or even toxic wild oysters for many reasons. The most logical reason was that in the days before refrigeration, shellfish were more likely to spoil in the heat.

The old rule of thumb was to eat oysters only in the months with the letter R in their names, because in colder weather, oysters would not spoil as quickly. Today, however, refrigeration keeps them fresh, and oysters can be harvested year-round.

TOXINS

History proves eating raw oysters is unsafe for certain groups of people because some raw oysters contain bacteria or viruses that can cause disease.

The abundance of *Vibrio vulnificus,* a potentially deadly bacterium in Gulf oysters that causes vibrosis, has been linked to warmer water temperature. *V. vulnificus* can cause severe illness and death in people with certain underlying medical conditions. Even though it has little or no effect on the healthiest people, slurping raw oysters from the Gulf during the summer months, especially in August, is somewhat risky. A similar bacterium, *V. parahaemolyticus,* can also cause food poisoning. Walsh found that even though Vibrio bacteria primarily occur in the Gulf of Mexico, "raw shellfish consumed in the warm summer months have sickened people in Washington State and as far north as Alaska."

There is no way to tell the difference between a contaminated oyster and one that is not contaminated by looking at it. However, if the oyster has a shrink-wrapped band around it, that means it has been treated for Vibrio bacteria.

Another interesting phenomenon seen in recent decades is red tide. This is a vast bloom of red algae that collects along coastlines when the waters are warming, more commonly seen in August and into September. Red tide causes eye irritations in humans and spreads toxins that are soaked up by all shellfish, including oysters, clams, and mussels. The Gulf of Mexico warms quicker and longer than the Pacific in the summer months. Handling procedures and updated harvesting regulations for red tide invasion in all five Gulf states are in place to ensure public safety.

The New Encyclopedia of Southern Culture, Volume 7 *Foodways* (2007) says:

> Oysters are susceptible to bio-toxins in the water. State and federal agencies monitor and approve oyster beds that are safe for commercial harvesting. Public health safety is always the number one concern. Proper handling protocol for oysters sold to restaurants, seafood markets, and urban area grocery stores must be commercially harvested and from properly licensed dealers and processors. As a result, oysters are subject to strictly enforced regulations intended to eliminate such potential hazards.

GULF COAST POST-HARVESTING TECHNIQUES FOR WILD OYSTERS

Along the Gulf Coast, and weather permitting, wild oysters are harvested every day. They are then refrigerated, or iced, in the proper time-allotment right out of water, and tagged to denote the harvest area and with a specific landing timeframe before being picked up by certified dealers. The dealers use refrigerated trucks to transport them to processing facilities, restaurants, and retailers. This reduces the risk for incorrect handling.

There are four bacteria treatment methods currently in place and available along the Gulf Coast for wild-harvested oysters. These are commercial, government-inspected processes devised to reduce your risk completely. But oyster-eaters beware, the process is not for the on-the-half-shell purist. It was designed to satisfy the Food and Drug Administration (FDA) by reducing Vibrio bacteria to non-detectable levels in our beloved Gulf oysters. Perhaps the biggest difference between purchasing treated oysters and non-treated oysters is that raw oysters straight from the boat remain alive until they are shucked and eaten. Three of these treatments kill the oyster and one does not. Nevertheless, Gulf Coast oyster bars and restaurants mostly stick to traditional untreated raw oysters, with many chefs, ostreaphiles, and consumers saying that there is a noticeable difference in taste when eating bacteria-treated processed oysters.

Here are the treatment methods:

- AmeriPure Oyster Co. of Franklin, Louisiana took the lead, founding the **Heat-Cool Pasteurization (HCP)** process for oysters in 1995, and using a signature AmeriPure rubber band for zero possibility of opening during the process. This is a patented process in which oysters are heated on trays in warm water to 124°F for 20 minutes, and then dipped in 40°F cold water for 15 minutes.

- Mike Voisin of Motivatit Seafood in Louisiana and his family research team discovered and patented a quite different bacterial treatment process in 1999. Their **High-Pressure Pasteurization (HPP)** process essentially deactivates the Vibrio bacteria at the molecular level by subjecting the oysters to intense water pressure. Oysters are placed into a cylinder that goes into a high-pressure water chamber. Water is then pumped into the chamber surrounding the cylinder for three minutes, exerting pressures of 35,000 to 40,000 pounds per square inch. Oysters, kept shut with the signature gold rubber band, are kept under this immense pressure for 3 minutes.

- Grady Leavins, a resilient Apalachicola oyster-fisherman transplant and visionary, developed **Individual Quick Freezing (IQF)**, in which half-shell oysters are rapidly frozen and then stored until consumption. In 2004, the technology was in full-swing for what he coined the "Frosted Oyster": an oyster that has been automatically shucked and then flash-frozen with liquid nitrogen.

- **Low-Dose Gamma Irradiation (LDG)** is the only process that does not kill the oyster. The process itself was developed more than 50 years ago, but testing on oysters didn't begin until the early 2000s. In preparation for irradiation, oysters are first individually rubber banded, boxed, and wrapped to secure onto a pallet. Pallets are fork-lifted onto refrigerated trucks and shipped to Gateway America for treatment, and then trucked back to the processor for distribution. The Mississippi facility is located at the Gulfport-Biloxi International Airport and is specially equipped for treating foods in this manner to ensure public safety. LDG is often considered the preferred method since it is less invasive, and unlike the other three methods, it kills just the bacteria and not the oyster.

Gulf oysters are at their best, most opaque, crispest, and plumpest in the cold-water months, which is why we traditionally associate the winter and early spring months as prime oyster time.

Magnolia Bluff Oysters on the half shell from Pensacola Bay Oyster Co.

That has been proven. However, unless there are bay closures in place by state agencies, then the water is considered healthy and it is open season, year-round. Additionally, in the Gulf Coast culture, cooked oysters are as equally significant as raw oysters. Since the 17th century, fresh oysters were eaten raw. Eventually, large big-bellied oysters were being cooked with roasted fowl, stewed with herbs and spices, roasted, or baked in pies. Keeping this tradition in mind, remember that Vibrio bacteria are destroyed by cooking—if there is any concern upon purchase, ask to have your oysters roasted, steamed, grilled, baked, or broiled, or purchase oysters that have been treated in one of the above ways. Don't restrict yourself from enjoying oysters year-round.

SHUCKING OYSTERS

PREPARATION

Wet a kitchen towel and wring it out well. Spread the damp towel flat on a work surface. Place a pie pan on the towel with a wooden puck or raised surface in the center for shucking. The pie pan will catch any spilled juices, which can be used in recipes that call for oyster liquor. If you prefer to shuck oysters in your hand, I recommend using a sturdy glove or steel-mesh glove.

Rinse the oysters with water to remove any sand or silt.

Next, select an oyster knife that is approximately 3 inches long with a pointed tip. This is important because smaller oysters have a small apex hinge and a thin but sturdy shell. Thicker knives with a dull point work best on larger wild oysters that require more force to open.

1 Place the oyster on the raised surface, cup side down. Fold a small dish towel to fit your hand and firmly hold the oyster in place. Next, insert the knife deep into the hinge with a slight twisting motion as shown. Be careful and go slow. Wiggle the blade until you feel the knife set. Do not try to open just yet.

2 Once the knife is set, push, turn, and apply medium torque to pop open the hinge.

3 When the hinge is popped, use your fingers to pry up the top shell (also called the cap).

4 Hold the shell open and slide the blade against the cap, gently dragging and jiggling the knife to scrape the shell from the adductor muscle. Remove and save the shell.

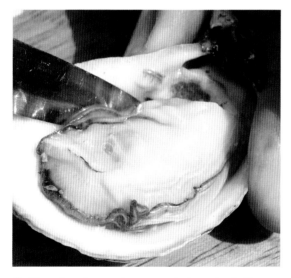

5 Now that the cap is removed, clean the knife tip on the towel, and then slide blade under oyster meat to remove from bottom adductor muscle. Touch the meat gently and you will feel it release. Do not puncture the oyster meat. Once meat is loosened, use tip of the knife to remove any grit or new shell growth around the meat and on edges.

6 The oyster has been shucked. Set the oyster in its shell directly onto ice or a tray.

OYSTER FARM PROFILES

Throughout this book, you will find profiles on Gulf Coast oyster farms I was able to visit and explore. In Florida, Alabama, and Louisiana, we grow the tastiest, most pristine oysters from seed to final growth in less than one year. I have documented information and photographs of specific farms from these states, but here is some general information about the oyster growing culture and processes in each state.

ALABAMA

"Alabama's reefs are known to have decreased dramatically in the last century because of overharvest and declining water quality. A massive effort funded by the National Oceanic and Atmospheric Administration and state officials has begun to restore vast areas of reef that had been lost," says Ben Raines, in his 2012 article titled *Wild Oyster Reefs in Mobile Bay and the Mississippi Sound Are Rare, Precious, and Delicate.* "Restoration projects of Alabama reefs include Coffee Island

Auburn University Marine Center work boat on Dauphin Island, Alabama.

in the Mississippi Sound, in Heron Bay, and in Mobile Bay, funded primarily through fine money associated with the 2010 Gulf oil spill. The progress on the Gulf Coast is seen as a model for how to restore oysters." In 2017, new lines and gear are now installed for Grand Bay Oyster Park, which will be used for both commercial operations and research.

On the other side of Mobile Bay from Pensacola, Florida, is Dauphin Island. I discovered this wonderful coastal town in 2015 when I attended my first Oyster Symposium. Dauphin Island is not only a fishing and summer resort, but is also home to the Auburn University Shellfish Lab. The Sea Lab, as they call it, is where Bill Walton and his team hatch the oyster seeds that are the bulk of all the oyster seeds grown and sold throughout the Southeast.

The bay is accessible from Mississippi Sound through a privately marked and dredged channel and is also open to Mobile Bay through an inlet protected by a jetty close to Pelican Point. This geographical proximity makes it ideal for growing oysters. The region was "conditionally approved" for growing and harvesting oysters by the Alabama Department of Public Health. Dauphin Island Bay is a shallow bay at the east end of Dauphin Island between Dauphin Island Bridge and Little Dauphin Island. In this location, oyster riparian rights are successfully being obtained to allow waterfront landowners locations for establishing off-bottom oyster farms.

With all the excitement about alternative oyster-growing, the demand for seed is exceeding the supply for other neighboring states like Florida. Alabama currently leads in single-seed production for the Gulf Coast states, producing millions of larvae and seeds.

Massacre Island Oyster Co. and Mobile Bay Oyster Co., located on the Mississippi Sound-Dauphin Island, and Murder Point Oyster Co. at Grand Bay are three of the 12 commercial oyster growers in operation throughout the Mobile Bay region. Bill Walton recently told me that two new farm permits have been issued, which means that 14 oyster growers will be in operation by the time this book is published. I wish that I could have visited all the oyster farms and met all the farmers in Alabama. Unfortunately, that was not possible, but they're on my oyster bucket list.

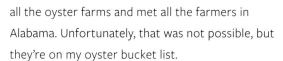

Shucking and tasting Mobile Bay Oyster Co. oysters straight from an oyster bag in a flipped submerged floating cage on Dauphin Island, Alabama, with Bill Walton.

Current Alabama Aquaculture Zones

Area I: Mobile Bay and Mississippi Sound
Area II: Grand Bay and Portersville Bay
Area III: Bon Secour Bay

FLORIDA

Florida's river and spring systems converge with the Gulf of Mexico, creating a unique balance between fresh and salt water, and making it one of the most fertile estuarine areas in the world. These waters are home to more than 300 living species, including the beloved oyster, where nutrient-rich phytoplankton are their lifeblood. In recent years, many of Florida's formerly degraded, natural oyster reefs have been restored: from St. Lucie Estuary to the Northwest Fork of the Loxahatchee River to a more recent reef restoration project in Pensacola's Escambia Bay.

Attempts have been made to restore all reefs as functioning ecosystems, providing many benefits for humans and the environment. Of course, oyster reefs provide essential habitat structures for many forms of marine life: shrimp, clams, crabs, snails, and a variety of recreationally important fish such as gag grouper, gray snapper, redfish, and sheepshead. That's what a healthy ecosystem does and it can have far-reaching, long-term benefits for neighboring ecosystems.

Bottom-culture oyster-farming has been promoted in various forms and shaped by varying laws for more than 100 years. In the 21st century, state-permitted water column leases have been approved to make way for off-bottom basket farming. A few who oppose this somewhat alien technique have attempted to physically sabotage the process. I strongly believe that off-bottom farming enables fishermen and their families a way to stay on the water by simply retraining them to the already familiar cultivating and harvesting techniques that previous generations have done for decades.

State officials have recommended that oyster aquaculture be operated on an even larger scale. As a top-priority issue to accelerate oyster recovery, entrepreneurs are encouraged to take a leap of faith and stimulate the creation of new jobs. Early in 2017, there were approximately 150 leases granted and only half of them are in use. Where is that poster of Uncle Sam wearing waders? As you can surmise, Florida is just getting started!

As you can see from the list below, Florida's Gulf of Mexico coastline is strewn with readily available oyster aquaculture zones. Yet, only a handful of bays and river estuaries are in full operation.

Current Florida Aquaculture Zones (subject to modifications)

Escambia County: Escambia Bay, East Bay
Franklin County: Alligator Harbor
Wakulla County: Apalachee Bay area, Oyster Bay, Skipper Bay
Dixie County: Horseshoe, Long Bar, Shired Reef, Piney Island

Magnolia Bluff location (Pensacola Bay Oyster Co.), off Scenic Highway 90 in Pensacola, Florida.

Levy County: Derricks, Pelican Reef (with Big Reef), Gulf Jackson, Dog Island East, Dog Island North, Dog Island, Corrigan's Reef, Corrigan's North
Charlotte County: Gasparilla Sound, North Piney Island, South Piney Island
Collier County: Cape Romano, Whitehorse Key
Palm Bay County: Volusia Bay, Body A, Body C
Brevard County: Body F and Indian River

LOUISIANA

In the mid-1800s, Croatian fisherman and their families began migrating to America for the first time. After arriving to the New World, many found their way to Louisiana, which turned out to be the perfect home for them to use their fishing skills. Louisiana is still recognized world-wide for its numerous wetlands and waterways, and its shrimping, fishing, crabbing, and oystering are still widespread. One such Croatian fisherman was John Popich, who started P&J Oyster Co. to distribute bottom-cultivated oysters. It is now the nation's oldest continuously working oyster house.

In recent years, Louisiana's oyster production has been compromised by saltwater intrusion due to coastal erosion. This has resulted in increased predators and a subsequent decrease in bottom-cultivated oyster production. One of the best ways to impede coastal erosion is to have oyster reefs firmly embedded into the ecosystem. Knowing this, the state of Louisiana has invested millions into reef restoration and coastal rebuilding.

As an alternative solution, cage-grown oysters are being used since they are protected from predators. This allows the oysters to be grown in areas where they can no longer reproduce in a wild setting and can place them in estuaries otherwise perfectly suited for oyster growing. The major keys to growing a delicious bayou-dipped oyster in Louisiana are to find a nutrient-rich current and knowing how to "chase the salinity." Beyond these seemingly simple tasks, the hardest part is finding a common ground between the fishermen who live, know, and work the estuaries, and the many conservationists who focus on long-term rebuilding. Fortunately, this struggle has been made easier by the likes of Oyster Specialist John Supan from LSU, the Godfather of the triploid oyster. He and others in the field have been instrumental in the search for alternative oyster growing methods. Over the years, Supan researched the aquaculture methods of other oyster-growing regions to arrive at a process for breeding triploid oysters. As discussed earlier, since triploid oysters don't spawn, they reach market size quicker than those that do. Supan sees off-bottom cultivation as a way to accomplish the goals of both sides of the debate during the last decade. But don't become too complacent with the notion that off-bottom oyster farming can trump Mother Nature and all her surprises—it's no surprise to me that Supans's favorite question to off-bottom oyster farming entrepreneurs is, "What's your hurricane plan?"

Now here's the skinny on the industry in Louisiana. Native oyster harvesting parishes consist of private leases and some 30 public areas extending hundreds of miles across southern Louisiana, which are sanctioned and carefully regulated by the state. According to the Louisiana Wild Life Fisheries and Oyster Task Force, the state maintains almost 1.7 million acres of public areas, and there are also approximately 400,000 acres of privately owned leases. These oyster

Hand oyster-shucking station at Bon Secour Fisheries in Bon Secour, Alabama.

beds are nestled in a maze of estuarine channels accessible only by boat. The oysters are mostly dredged (i.e., scraped by machine) or sometimes picked by tongs for harvesting.

Currently, there are three off-bottom oyster farmers with active leases at Caminada Bay for the entire state of Louisiana; however, leasing zones have been expanded and new leases have been approved for the area.

Louisiana also produces millions of seeds, leaning on the Michael C. Voisin Oyster Hatchery facility located at the Department of Wildlife and Oyster Hatchery Building on Grand Isle. Louisiana chooses to keep seeds in-state by providing them to their own Grand Isle oyster farmers for reseeding their own reefs.

48

38

46

40

CHAPTER 2

DROPS, MIGNONETTES, MISTS & HOT SAUCES

LEMON-OLIVE OIL MIST
with RED PEPPER FLAKES

——— Makes about 2 ½ ounces ———

Slurping oysters in the purest form requires little adornment, particularly for the premium or cocktail oyster on the half shell. In fact, some oyster lovers snub the idea of adding anything more than a squeeze of lemon or a splash of hot sauce, and perhaps a simple cracker. On certain days, the harvested oyster has a perfect salinity, ranging from approximately 15 to 20 parts per thousand (ppt), and needs nothing at all to adorn it. Freshwater flow, location, wind direction, rain, and harvest depth dictate salinity levels, and when salinity falls below 14 ppt, oysters will have a mild flavor. Here is another great way to add a subtle and simple flavor enhancer— just a spritz of lemon-olive oil mixture, a pinch of heat, and depending on the oyster's brine content, a pinch of sea salt.

½ ounce extra-virgin olive oil

1 ounce fresh lemon juice, from 1 to 2 lemons

1 ounce bottled water

Pinch sea salt (optional)

Pinch dried red pepper flakes

Shuck and taste the liquor of your premium oyster. If briny, do not add sea salt to the mixture. In a small mixing bowl, stir together olive oil, lemon juice, water, and a pinch of sea salt (if needed). Use a small funnel to pour the mixture into a small 2 to 4 ounce sanitized spray bottle. Shake well, mist over chilled oysters on the half shell, and then top each oyster with a pinch of red pepper flakes. Serve right away.

WATERMELON HABANERO
HOT SAUCE

—— Makes about 2 cups ——

In the South, watermelon is the quintessential food for picnics on hot summer days. Another wonderful treat is slurping down chilled cocktail oysters with a cold craft beer (or two). So why not bring the two foods together? In this recipe, the watermelon juice blend is cool and refreshing, countered with the spicy heat of a habanero pepper. This topping will provide a perfect balance of fire and sweetness to your oysters—truly the best of both worlds. And if you have some vodka lying about, add a splash (or two) to the watermelon juice mix while it's still in the blender.

2 cups seedless ripe watermelon, coarsely chopped

½ pint raspberries

1 medium shallot, coarsely chopped

½ small habanero pepper, seeded and coarsely chopped

¼ cup raspberry vinegar

1 teaspoon lime juice

3 small basil leaves

Freshly ground black pepper

Place watermelon, raspberries, shallot, habanero, vinegar, lime, and basil into blender. Cover, pulse, and run machine until mixture is smooth, about 10 seconds, and then transfer mixture to a small bowl. Cover with plastic wrap and place in refrigerator for 2 hours. Just before serving, add a few turns from the peppermill over top and stir. Serve in a small bowl with a small spoon alongside premium Gulf Coast oysters on the half shell, and serve immediately.

Note: If you're a fan of the spicy habanero pepper, you may choose to add more of the pepper. For us regular folks, half a pepper offers plenty heat for this sauce.

BERRY & SMOKY JALAPEÑO MIGNONETTE

Makes about 2 cups

Nowadays, variations on components of mignonette sauce served with oysters are as diverse as relish or salsa recipes for pork, chicken, beef, or fish. This recipe provides a tasty foundation for creating a one-of-a-kind mignonette sauce for oysters. Pairing ripe seasonal berries with smoky chipotle peppers in adobo and fresh chilies will give you a strong sense of how to balance a range of bold-flavored ingredients. A good rule of thumb for any simple, easy-to-make, masterpiece recipe like this is to combine *sweet and spicy* with vinegar, shallots, and cracked pepper. The smoky and herbal notes will do the rest.

½ teaspoon minced chipotles in adobo sauce

½ teaspoon additional adobo sauce

½ cup raspberry vinegar

½ cup seasoned rice wine vinegar

1 tablespoon seeded and minced jalapeño

2 tablespoons minced shallot

Freshly ground black pepper

½ pint fresh seasonal berries (such as blueberries or raspberries)

12 small leaves picked from 3 mint sprigs for garnish

In a small mixing bowl, stir together the chipotle, adobo sauce, raspberry vinegar, seasoned rice vinegar, jalapeño, and shallot. Taste; season with black pepper. Place in a tightly sealed container in the refrigerator for 4 hours or overnight. Garnish each chilled cocktail oyster with a teaspoon of the sauce with berries and small mint leaves. Serve immediately.

MAGNOLIA BLUFF MIGNONETTE

——— Makes about 1 cup ———

Pensacola is notorious for adapting to its settings. Some 500 years ago, a massive estuary system evolved from the sediment carried down from the Appalachian Mountains, creating present day Escambia Bay. The same flow deposited the oval grains of white quartz sand that shaped the Santa Rosa Island bay systems and formed our beautiful white beaches. The bays became the source for bountiful seafood like oysters, which in turn help to clean the bays by filtering the water and creating a healthy habitat for all marine life. Right now, Gulf Coast hatchery-produced oyster seeds are being raised off-bottom, and can be seen in their floating cages overlooking Magnolia Bluff along Pensacola's scenic highway. I prepared this mignonette sauce to accompany Magnolia Bluff Oysters, Pensacola's premium comeback oyster, and for the grand opening event for Pensacola Bay Oyster Co. Oysters are back in our bay!

⅓ cup white balsamic vinegar

⅓ cup seasoned rice wine vinegar

¼ raspberry vinegar

1 lime, juiced

1 jalapeño pepper, seeded and minced

3 tablespoons minced shallot

Freshly cracked black pepper

2 tablespoons small-chopped cilantro leaves

In a small mixing bowl, stir together the balsamic vinegar, rice vinegar, raspberry vinegar, lime juice, jalapeño, and shallot. Stir, taste, and season with black pepper. Place in a tightly sealed container in the refrigerator for 2 hours or overnight. Just before serving, add the cilantro, stir, and then spoon over chilled cocktail oysters. Serve right away.

MUSTARD SEED MIGNONETTE

Makes about 1½ cups

Cooking should be a curious and enjoyable endeavor, pretty much the same as discovering that favorite craft oyster or beer. Creating your own basic mustard from scratch involves a fun and simple process of soaking mustard seeds in vinegar, beer, or wine for two days, and then processing it to the desired consistency. Many people never think about making mustard. Nevertheless, it's quite easy.

For this preparation, the mustard seeds will bloom enough in 8 hours to develop a pungent flavor, slight heat, and a caviar-like pop, and will be the centerpiece of the sauce. Inspired by the classic pairing of mustard seeds and dill for pickle making, fresh dill became the obvious herbal choice for complementing the malty sweetness and spiciness of the mustard grains.

2 tablespoons yellow (white) mustard seeds

2 tablespoons brown mustard seeds

½ cup champagne vinegar

¼ cup apple cider vinegar

2 tablespoons minced shallot

2 tablespoons seeded and minced jalapeño pepper

½ cup amber lager beer

2 tablespoons small-chopped fresh dill

Freshly ground black pepper

In a small bowl, combine mustard seeds, champagne vinegar, apple cider vinegar, shallot, and jalapeño pepper. Seal bowl tightly with plastic wrap, and then place in refrigerator overnight. Just before serving, add the beer, stir, and add the dill. Taste; adjust seasoning with pepper. Spoon over chilled cocktail oysters and serve immediately.

TART APPLE MIGNONETTE

—— Makes about 1 cup ——

Granny Smith, queen of the tart apples, is easy to find and known for being used in a wide spectrum of culinary dishes. In fact, these apples are perfect for juicing and immediately drinking with nothing added at all. Frozen, they also make excellent sorbet and granita (i.e., flavored ice). Their thick skins enable them to store for long periods of time, and although they tend to ripen best in warmer climates where they get a significant amount of sunshine, they can be found everywhere. The brilliant green and refreshingly tart juice makes an excellent component to mignonette sauce.

½ cup fresh tart apple juice, from 1 Granny Smith apple

4 tablespoons apple cider vinegar

¼ cup white balsamic vinegar

1 tablespoon fresh lime juice

¼ cup finely chopped Granny Smith apple

2 tablespoons minced shallot

2 tablespoons finely chopped cilantro leaves

Freshly ground black pepper

In a small mixing bowl, stir together the fresh apple juice, apple cider vinegar, white balsamic vinegar, lime juice, apple, shallot, and cilantro. Taste; adjust seasoning with pepper. Place in a tightly sealed container in the refrigerator for 2 hours or overnight. Spoon over chilled cocktail oysters just before serving.

Note: *Use a home juice extractor to juice the apple. If a juice extractor is not available, omit the juice from the recipe, triple the white balsamic vinegar, and add the juice of another lime.*

—— Oyster Farm ——

MOBILE OYSTER CO.

ALABAMA

Many of the top restaurants throughout the Southeast recognize Cullan Duke's Mobile Oyster Co. and its Isle Dauphine oysters as the best. Cullan grew up sailing and fishing in Mobile Bay and around the island, and now lives and practices law in Mobile, while also working the waters that were once his childhood playground. He happened on the idea of oyster farming by accident. His interest began in 2012 while chatting with Bill Walton about a stretch of water he'd discovered off the island during his law days. The company he started is now Mobile Oyster Co.

On my trip to Dauphin Island, Cullan and his wife, Nicolette, were unable to meet up with us, but Bill Walton was kind enough to fill in for them that day. He guided me and photographer Bill Strength to their sand parking lot on the extreme west end of Dauphin Island and walked us out to the floating oyster cages.

Shucking and tasting Mobile Oyster Co. oysters straight from an oyster bag in a flipped submerged floating cage on Dauphin Island, Alabama, with Bill Walton (all).

We waded in chest-high water and saw some oysters being staged for harvest. When we made our way back to the beach, Bill had to return to work at the Sea Lab. Just then, a young farm manager named Aaron Fowler pulled up in a white pick-up truck. He had a cooler filled with some gorgeous white-shelled, premium oysters in a bright red bag. They had been freshly tagged from an earlier morning harvest. He asked us if we had time to do another quick tour. Easy answer, right?

We helped him launch a small, slightly beat-up johnboat with "Miss Cate" printed on its bright teal hull. Aaron explained that Cullan and his helpers routinely rowed it out to his cages a few hundred yards off-shore in Mississippi Sound to check on his crop. Aaron said, "Have a seat," and pulled us around the farm in his boat using a tattered rope. He even gave us a closer look at some triploid oyster seeds.

Isle Dauphine Oysters, bagged and tagged (top left); staging Isle Dauphine oyster seeds (top right); a mature Isle Dauphine oyster (bottom left).

CUCUMBER MIGNONETTE

—— *Makes about 1 cup* ——

Mignonette sauces complement the brightness of any oyster on the half shell. And cucumbers are excellent for adding freshness, elegance, and a delicate crunch to any mignonette. Cucumbers have been used in spicy Arabic, Indian, and French dishes for centuries. Plucked from creeping vines, these fruits that are used as vegetables are on the market all year-round, but are most available and best during the summer. We grow seed cucumber varieties such as Kirby in Florida; however, seedless English cucumbers are available everywhere.

1 cup seasoned rice wine vinegar

6 tablespoons peeled and finely chopped English cucumber

2 tablespoons minced shallot

2 tablespoons small-chopped fresh dill

Freshly ground black pepper

In a small mixing bowl, stir together the vinegar, cucumber, shallot, and dill. Taste; adjust seasoning with pepper. Place in a tightly sealed container in the refrigerator for 2 hours or overnight. Spoon over chilled cocktail oysters just before serving.

RUBY RED MIGNONETTE

—— *Makes about 1 ½ cups* ——

How did mignonette become a sauce for oysters? As a chef, that's a question I have been asking for decades. It's certainly not one of the five classic French mother sauces, and it's not a traditional French cold sauce, but could be considered a relative of vinaigrette. The French translation and morphed American use of the word now often refers to anything small. The term *mignonette* can be found in the *New Larousse Gastronomic* (printed in English in 1977) and is the French name given for coarsely ground pepper. For decades, the sauce has been touted as a tasty and vinegary accompaniment to raw oysters; but today and around the country it most often translates as a condiment made with minced shallots, cracked pepper, and vinegar.

⅓ cup white balsamic vinegar

⅓ cup raspberry vinegar

⅓ cup Ruby Red grapefruit juice

1 Ruby Red grapefruit, supremed
(see note) and small chopped

2 tablespoons minced shallot

Freshly ground black pepper

In a small mixing bowl, stir together the white balsamic vinegar, raspberry vinegar, grapefruit juice, chopped grapefruit, and shallot. Taste; adjust seasoning with pepper. Place in a tightly sealed container in the refrigerator for 2 hours or overnight. Spoon sauce over chilled cocktail oysters just before serving.

Note: Supreming a citrus fruit is a French technique in which the ends of the round fruit are cut away, enabling the fruit to sit flat; the peel is then sliced away with a utility knife, removing the peel and pith, leaving only the pure fruit segments.

SAZERAC MIGNONETTE

——— Makes about ½ cup ———

There is no place is more famous for oysters on the Gulf of Mexico than New Orleans! And nothing could be better than sipping a hand-crafted Sazerac cocktail at The Sazerac Bar inside The Roosevelt Hotel—a New Orleans landmark. Nowadays, nothing screams oysters louder than mignonette, a sauce that began topping oysters on the half shell on the city tables of the South as early as the 1980s. I did an adaptation of my own to the 1850s cocktail using the classic ingredients of a Sazerac, and then transformed it into a shallotlike and slightly sweet sauce to spoon over cocktail oysters. It's like slurping an oyster coated with a sweet vinegary Sazerac. A toast to a new Gulf Coast classic!

½ ounce absinthe (or Pernod)

½ cup cubed ice

1 teaspoon granulated sugar

1 ounce rye whiskey

3 dashes Peychaud's bitters

1 ounce raspberry vinegar

1 lemon peel

2 tablespoons minced shallot

Freshly ground black pepper

In a cocktail shaker, add absinthe, ice, sugar, whiskey, bitters, vinegar, and lemon peel. Cap the shaker and shake well 24 times. Remove lemon peel and cut into thin strips for garnish. Pour into a small bowl; add shallot and pepper. Spoon sauce over chilled cocktail oysters just before serving.

CEVICHE, CRUDO & CHILLED TOPPINGS

MEYER LEMON SUPREME
& HOT SAUCE

Makes topping for about 1 dozen oysters on the half shell

The classic combination for savoring oysters on the half shell along the Gulf Coast is saltine crackers, hot sauce, and lemon. That trio is all you'll ever need. But feel free to add some prepared horseradish if you want to turn it up a notch! In this simple recipe, lemon segments will add a punch of citrus to each bite. Pure lemon meat and drops of hot sauce contribute their quintessential flavorings, yet you will still be able to recognize the taste of the oyster's merroir.

2 large Meyer lemons, supremed (see page 54)

Hot sauce (your favorite brand or homemade)

1 sleeve saltine crackers

Place one lemon supreme segment on top of each oyster. Add drops of hot sauce. Serve right away on crushed ice with crackers on the side.

MY CEVICHE SAUCE

Makes topping for about 1 dozen oysters on the half shell

Ceviche is the seafood favorite of south Florida and has now become popularized along Florida's north Gulf Coast. Peruvian fishermen often pickled fresh-caught fish at sea to feed themselves during their fishing excursions, as is now done by lionfish divers on the hunt and fishermen alike. Ceviche is typically made of raw fish and/or partially cooked shellfish marinated in citrus juices. Renowned chef Norman Van Aken noted in his *A Word on Food* series article "The Mysterious Origins of Ceviche" that Peruvian food scholar Juan José Vega claimed Moorish slaves introduced a dish to Peru called Sei-vech, made of fish marinated in the juice of Ceuta lemons, which they brought with them from North Africa.

1 Ruby Red grapefruit, supremed (see preparation)

1 orange, supremed (see preparation)

½ ripe mango, finely diced (see preparation)

2 limes (1 zested, both juiced)

1 teaspoon minced shallot

1 jalapeño pepper, seeded and minced

½ red bell pepper, finely minced

2 tablespoons finely chopped cilantro

1 tablespoon extra-virgin olive oil

Pinch sea salt

Pinch ground cumin

Pinch ground coriander

TO PREPARE THE CITRUS SUPREME: Cut the ends off the grapefruit and orange. Place them flat side-down on a cutting board. In downward slices, following the natural curve of the fruit, cut peel and pith off the fruit. Hold over a small mixing bowl and cut between each section to remove the segments, discarding the stringy portion as you go. Collect segments and juice as they fall into the bowl. Squeeze out any remaining juice from the membrane and discard.

TO PREPARE THE MANGO: Hold the mango flat on a cutting board and use a sharp knife to remove the ends. Stand on end and cut between the skin and the mango meat lengthwise. Cut over the top of the oblong large seed to remove the mango top half. Cut into long thin strips, finely dice, and add to the mixing bowl.

FURTHER PREPARATION: Add lime juice and zest, shallot, peppers, cilantro, olive oil, salt, cumin, and coriander. Stir with a spoon to blend and break up citrus sections. Place in refrigerator and let chill for 1 hour.

TO SERVE: Spoon chilled sauce over top of freshly shucked premium oysters on the half shell. Or for large oysters, place freshly shucked oysters with their liquor into a medium Mason jar or serving dish. Cover oysters with ceviche sauce and stir to blend. Let cook by acidulation for a minimum of 3 hours in the refrigerator. Serve in their bottom shell or in cocktail glasses over crushed ice.

Note: My ceviche sauce is designed to accentuate the raw oyster; however, an overnight stay in the refrigerator would cook the oyster completely by acidulation.

SESAME SEAWEED SALAD
with FLYING FISH ROE & CRISPY WONTONS

——— *Makes topping for about 1 dozen oysters on the half shell* ———

Japanese seaweed salad, or sesame seaweed salad, is made with hiyashi wakame. Although wakame is most commonly sold dried, it's my understanding that hiyashi wakame is made with fresh wakame stems. There are many different suppliers of seaweed salads, including some who customize orders for their clients, which explains why different restaurants carry different salads. I suggest researching brands and suppliers until you find one you're happy with. Be sure to analyze the ingredient label carefully; some suppliers use food colorings and preservatives, while others do not. I love using seasoned seaweed salad with oysters because it adds yet another taste of the sea.

2 cups vegetable oil

6 square wonton wrappers, cut into thin long strips

½ teaspoon black sesame seeds

½ teaspoon white sesame seeds

2 ounces sesame seaweed salad

1 ounce orange tobiko caviar (flying fish roe)

Preheat heat oil to 350°F in a 9-inch cast iron skillet. Add one wonton strip to test the fry oil. When oil is shimmering and the wonton begins to fry up crispy, add all the wonton strips and stir until lightly brown, about 2 minutes. Remove wontons from the hot oil with a slotted spoon and let drain on a paper towel–lined plate until needed.

Place sesame seeds in a small non-stick skillet over medium-low heat for 3 to 4 minutes. Shake frequently until white sesame seeds turn light brown and aromatic. Remove pan from the stove and transfer toasted sesame seeds to a plate until needed.

Use a fork to grab, twist, and portion the seaweed salad over half of each raw oyster. Add a generous pinch of tobiko caviar to each oyster. Top oyster with pieces of crispy wontons and a pinch of toasted sesame seeds over top. Serve right away on crushed ice.

SALMON PEARLS & SERRANO PEPPERS

Makes topping for about 1 dozen oysters on the half shell

Several varieties of fish eggs, or roe, are available along the Gulf and Atlantic Coasts, including mullet, some species of sturgeon (such as hackleback), and Alabama paddlefish. Tobiko caviar, or flying fish roe, a brightly colored roe seen in sushi bars, is affordable and quite easy to find in grocery stores everywhere. Salmon roe, which comes from the Pacific Northwest, is a brilliant orange in color, the size of a pearl, and won't cost you the price of one! Of course, if you can get your hands on some high-end black or gold caviar such as beluga, osetra, sevruga, or sea urchin (a.k.a. uni), throw out some extra cash, spoon it over some premium medium-sized oysters, and let the combination blow your mind! To create more intense contrasting flavors and textures for this recipe, add thinly sliced serrano peppers to give the taste of the sea a spicy edge.

1 ounce salmon roe (or your favorite caviar)

1 serrano or jalapeño pepper, seeded and cut into 12 thin slices on a bias

1 lemon, cut into wedges

1 sleeve saltine crackers

Use a caviar spoon to top each oyster with the roe. Add one slice of pepper to each. Serve right away on crushed ice with lemon wedges and saltines.

COBIA CRUDO

with LEMON, OLIVE OIL & JALAPEÑO

Makes topping for about 1 dozen oysters on the half shell

Cool ceviches and crudos are the best ways to enjoy freshly caught fish in its purest form. Now sustainably farmed off the coast of Panama by Open Blue, cobia are shipped throughout the country and respected by chefs everywhere. Loved by Gulf fisherman and chefs alike, cobia are not only powerful swimmers and rugged fighters, but the meat is one of the finest you will ever put in your mouth. If chefs aren't out there fishing for cobia themselves, they'll be serving them up all season long. Here is an excellent recipe to try out after your next successful fishing trip that makes for a terrific topping for cocktail-size oysters.

8 ounces fresh sushi-quality cobia

Pinch coarse sea salt

1 teaspoon finely chopped fresh chives

1 teaspoon seeded and minced jalapeño

1 teaspoon minced shallot

1 tablespoon fresh lemon juice

2 tablespoons extra-virgin olive oil

Slice the fish across the grain into eight thin slices. Lay them flat on a clean cutting surface, dice small, and then season with a pinch of salt. Place the rest of the ingredients in a bowl, stir in the cobia, place in refrigerator, and let marinate for 15 minutes. Spoon chilled crudo over top of oysters on the half shell. Serve right away on crushed ice.

GROUPER CRUDO
with FENNEL & SERRANO HAM

Makes topping for about 1 dozen oysters on the half shell

Crudo is Italian for "uncooked," and refers to raw food. Eating oysters on their half shells is my favorite way to celebrate the taste of the bay from whence they came. Freshly caught yellow-edge grouper is one of my favorite Gulf treasures, and it is easy to find at the seafood market. Combine the two by adding a splash of simple Italian ingredients, and you'll wind up with flavors that not only complement the fish, but the oyster too. This is heaven in an oyster shell. The cool thing is that the unique individual flavors and textures are remarkably distinguishable in just a single bite.

8 ounces fresh sushi-quality yellow-edge grouper (see note)

Pinch coarse sea salt

3 tablespoons finely chopped fennel bulb; reserve fronds for garnish

1 slice thinly cut serrano or prosciutto ham, finely chopped

2 teaspoons fresh lemon juice

2 tablespoons extra-virgin olive oil

Freshly ground black pepper

Slice the fish across the grain into eight thin slices. Lay them flat on a clean cutting surface, dice small, and then season with a pinch of salt. Place fennel bulb, ham, lemon, and olive oil in a bowl and stir together. Stir in grouper, place mixture in refrigerator, and let marinate for 15 minutes. Spoon chilled crudo over top freshly shucked oysters. Garnish with fennel fronds. Serve right away on crushed ice.

Note: Place the fish in the freezer 20 minutes before slicing. Once firm, it'll be easier to slice through and the fish will cut into perfect small cubes.

Oyster Farm
MASSACRE ISLAND OYSTER RANCH
ALABAMA

Situated within the western gate of the Sunshine State, Pensacola is a mere 20-minute car ride from the Alabama state line. The first time I would have an up-close look at an off-bottom oyster farm was over in Alabama.

In October 2016, with perfect fall weather in play and after our informative tour of the impressive Dauphin Island AU Shellfish Laboratory Facility, Bill Walton was kind enough to lead me and photographer Bill Strength to a young aquaculturalist named Tyler Myers. Tyler is the founder and grower of Massacre Island Oyster Ranch and is an Auburn University graduate with a degree in Fisheries and Aquaculture. Tyler and his family also participated with Auburn University's research study to develop techniques for off-bottom oyster farming in the Gulf of Mexico.

Tyler's ranch was just a few miles down the island's main road and juts out in front their family beach home, which sits on the Mississippi sound side at the west end of Dauphin Island. Bill Walton handled the arrangements for our visit there. When we arrived at Tyler's ranch, he and his dad Steve were graciously waiting. They had a wooden table set on the water's edge. On it were a handful of iced oysters in a cooler, a shucker, and a proudly displayed copy of *Oysters: A Celebration in the Raw*, in which they were featured. Tyler put the oysters on the table—the shells were pristine. We shucked and tasted briny diploids that were deep-cupped and brimming with plump meat. He had my attention! I joined young Tyler in the water to see his oysters first-hand. We waded out to the

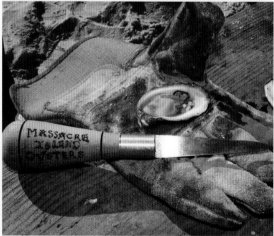

Massacre Island oyster farm, looking into Mississippi Sound (top). A freshly shucked Massacre Island oyster on Dauphin Island (bottom).

middle of some 30 floating cages and began to flip cages and pull out mesh bags filled with various stages of marketable oysters. Tyler explained, "I remember finding oyster shells all along this beach when I was a kid. We named our farm Massacre Island Oyster Ranch to keep the Island's rich history alive and pay tribute to the Island's original inhabitants." In the eyes of a child! Made me feel young again.

Oyster farmer and owner Tyler Myers pulling a bag from a floating cage to check growth of some of his diploid oysters (top). Tyler displays his Massacre Island oysters (bottom left). Cages, looking back onto Dauphin Island (bottom right).

SPICY TAMARI, CARROT SLAW &
FRIED CHICKEN SKIN FURIKAKE

——— *Makes topping for about 1 dozen oysters on the half shell* ———

Traditionally, ingredients used in cooked oyster recipes are ingredients of compatibility, such as sweetbreads, flavored butters, and soft cheeses. The new mindset is to combine ingredient components strongly contrasting in texture and flavor to give a one-bite wow factor to cooked or raw oyster recipes. At the 2016 Hangout Oyster Cook-Off, chef Jesse Huston of Saltine Oyster Bar in Jackson, Mississippi, created a raw oyster topping using pumpkin for kimchi and fried-chicken skins seasoned with furikake, resulting in an award-winning preparation for the raw oyster category. I enjoyed it so much I had to craft my own easy-to-replicate version featuring chicken skin and furikake.

CARROT SLAW

1 medium carrot, peeled and grated

3 tablespoons seasoned rice wine vinegar

1 teaspoon sriracha

Chicken skin (removed from 2 chicken breasts or thighs)

3 tablespoons vegetable oil

1 teaspoon katsuo fumi furikake (see note)

Pinch salt

SPICY TAMARI SYRUP

½ cup chicken broth (store bought or homemade)

¼ cup seasoned rice wine vinegar

¼ cup tamari or soy sauce

3 tablespoons molasses

½ teaspoon grated fresh ginger

1 jalapeño, seeded and minced

Note: Furikake is a dry Japanese sushi rice seasoning often consisting of sesame seeds, seaweed flakes, salt, and sugar. There are several types of furikake seasoning blends that can be found in Asian grocery stores or online. Look for one labeled "Katsuo Fumi Furikake" for this recipe, meaning that there are dried fish flakes included.

FOR CARROT SLAW: Combine the carrot, vinegar, and sriracha in a small bowl and place in refrigerator for 15 minutes. Remove the skin from the chicken and reserve the meat for another day's meal. Lay the skin out flat on a tray or dish and freeze for one hour. Cut skin into strips and place into a frying pan with the oil over medium heat for about 5 minutes until crispy. Place onto a paper towel–lined plate to drain. Season with furikake and a pinch of salt. Let cool completely to get crispy.

FOR SPICY TAMARI SYRUP: Combine chicken broth, vinegar, tamari or soy sauce, molasses, ginger, and jalapeño in a sauce pan and bring to a boil over high heat. Reduce the mixture at a rolling boil to ½ cup, about 7 to 10 minutes, creating a thin syruplike sauce. Remove from heat and set aside.

TO SERVE: Drizzle ½ teaspoon of the spicy tamari syrup over each raw oyster. Add a generous pinch of marinated carrot to each oyster. Top with pieces of seasoned fried chicken skins and another pinch of furikake over top. To enjoy the supple and crispy textures, serve right away on crushed ice.

LIONFISH CRUDO

with **TOBIKO CAVIAR & SRIRACHA**

—— *Makes topping for about 1 dozen oysters on the half shell* ——

I never take it for granted how fortunate I am to live and work just a few miles from the Gulf of Mexico. In support of eradicating the invasive lionfish from our Pensacola reefs, this past year Jackson's Steakhouse purchased a Florida saltwater license, which I now use to purchase fresh lionfish directly off dive boats of concerned lionfish hunters. My Pensacola diver-partner, Captain Andy Ross of Niuhi Dive Charters, is a lionfish hunter of the same mindset. He could easily ship off our local lionfish to metropolitan cites for big bucks, but believes that it should remain reasonably priced and enjoyed at restaurants within our own community.

6 ounces skinless lionfish fillets or mild fish such as yellowtail, flounder, or snapper

Pinch sea salt

1 ounce tobiko caviar (flying fish roe), natural or colored

Drops of sriracha

6 Thai chilies, reserved for garnishing

Using lionfish or the fish of your choice, lay the fillet flat on a clean cutting surface. Use a very sharp knife to slice the fish into eight thin slices, and then dice small, or, if you prefer, cut 12 thin slices of sashimi from the fillets on a bias, then place one slice over each oyster. Season with a pinch of salt. Use a small spoon to top each oyster with tobiko. Add one dot of sriracha over the tobiko. Serve right away on crushed ice. Garnish with the whole Thai chilies.

SCALLOP CRUDO
with SEVILLE ORANGE MOJO

Makes topping for about 1 dozen oysters on the half shell

During the first Spanish Period (1559 to 1561) in the Pensacola Bay area, the Spanish brought lemons, oranges, and limes with them to the New World. A specific variety of citrus, known as Seville orange, still grows in Historic Pensacola Village. The citrus is not eaten fresh because it's far too sour. The best use for a sour orange like this is in marinades, which is why it's such a perfect ingredient for this classic sour-orange mojo and scallop crudo. There's a great remote spot just east of Mexico Beach in Florida's Big Bend where the incredibly fun Florida Scallop & Music Festival takes place in Port St. Joe every September. Quality bay or sea scallops from any coast will work for this recipe.

½ teaspoon cumin seed, toasted (see note)

½ teaspoon whole coriander, toasted (see note)

1 teaspoon garlic, coarsely chopped

1 serrano or jalapeño pepper, seeded and minced

Pinch smoky paprika (La Chinata brand preferred)

Pinch sea salt

¾ cup pure olive oil

¼ cup fresh Seville orange juice (or ⅛ cup each navel orange and lime juice)

1 tablespoon sherry vinegar

1 tablespoon small-chopped cilantro leaves

4 to 6 ounces fresh large sea scallops, small diced, or bay scallops

In a mortar, mash the cumin, coriander, garlic, pepper, paprika, and salt. Use a rubber spatula to transfer the mixture to a medium-size metal mixing bowl. In a sauce pan, add olive oil and cook over medium heat for 3 to 4 minutes, until hot, but not shimmering. Pour this over the garlic mixture, stir, and let sit 15 minutes. Whisk in the orange juice, sherry vinegar, cilantro, and scallops. Refrigerate for a minimum of 1 hour. Spoon the mixture over top of premium oysters, and serve right away on crushed ice.

Notes: Shape up the scallops and place them on a pan in the freezer 40 minutes before slicing; it'll be easier to slice through.

Toasting spices can easily be done in a dry sauté pan. Gently warm the seeds over medium heat until they become aromatic and toasted. Turn them out onto a cool surface. Let cool before mashing.

82

88

93

CHAPTER 4

SOUPS, GUMBO & STEWS

OYSTER CHOWDER
with CREAMER POTATOES, KALE & CORN

———— 6 servings ————

Everything about this chowder is simply irresistible. The young-harvested, marble-sized, red creamer potatoes give the soup an earthy, sweet flavor, and provide a rustic appearance. Young and tender kale, such as red or green, cooks quickly in the gently simmering milk and cream, and is brimming with brilliant color and freshness. These wholesome flavors and textures are then paired with grilled corn-off-the-cob, delicately poached Gulf oysters, and toasted French bread for sopping. Now that's just plain sexy!

1 pound small white or red new potatoes, rinsed and halved or quartered

2 pints freshly shucked Gulf Coast oysters, with 1 cup liquor reserved

3 ears fresh sweet corn (enough to make 1½ cups shaved corn kernels)

2 tablespoons pure olive oil

4 tablespoons (½ stick) unsalted butter

1 cup small-chopped yellow onion

1 medium green pepper, seeded and small chopped

1 rib celery, small chopped

1 teaspoon minced garlic

½-pound coarsely chopped kale (thick ribs removed)

4 tablespoons all-purpose flour

3 cups milk

1 cup heavy cream

Kosher salt

Freshly ground black pepper

Hot sauce

1 baguette French bread, toasted

Place the cut potatoes in a 3-quart soup pot and cover with water. Turn heat to high and bring to a boil. Reduce heat and simmer gently until fork tender, about 20 minutes. Drain.

Strain oysters and reserve the liquor until needed. Preheat grill to medium-high. Shuck corn and remove silk. Dip a paper towel into the oil, rub oil all over the ears of corn, and then place on the grill over indirect heat. Turn every few minutes until the ears are charred all over, about 5 to 7 minutes. Remove from grill and let cool. Cut off the thick end of the cobs so the corn stands upright on your cutting board. Hold the top firmly and slice straight down the sides to remove kernels. Set corn kernels aside.

Melt the butter in the soup pot over medium heat. Add the onion, green pepper, celery, and garlic; stir until vegetables are tender and aromatic, about 5 minutes. Add the kale, stir, and cook for about 2 minutes or until the kale wilts. Sprinkle in flour and blend well. Add the potatoes, corn, milk, cream, and oyster liquor, increase heat to medium-high, and bring to a boil. Reduce heat to low and gently simmer for about 25 minutes.

Just before serving, add the oysters and stir. Let cook until the edges of the oysters begin to curl, about 2 to 3 minutes. Taste; adjust seasoning with salt, pepper, and hot sauce. Serve right away in large hot soup bowls with toasted French bread.

Note: If you don't have enough oyster liquor, add clam juice or water to reach the correct amount.

OYSTER & BRIE SOUP

———— 6 servings ————

I was schooled in seafood houses along the mid-Atlantic and upper East Coast. So, when I relocated in 1982 to Destin, Florida—the World's Luckiest Fishing Village—clams and oysters were never very far from my heart. In the years before moving to the Gulf Coast, I was first introduced to brie soup by a German chef. I can't quite remember where his recipe originated, but I do know that a similar recipe appeared in chef Paul Prudhomme's *Louisiana Kitchen,* printed in 1984. Nevertheless, I kept accurate notes, and his brie soup was a huge hit for our first menu at Les Saisons in Destin. Many years later, I crafted my own version using freshly shucked Gulf oysters, and each time I make it, it's better than the last. My rendition combines velvety brie cheese and supple Gulf oysters. I love everything about this soup.

BRIE CROUTON

1 small baguette, sliced into eight ¼-inch slices

8-ounce brie cheese wheel, cut into 6½-inch-thick slices to fit the baguette slices, rest reserved

SOUP

2 pints freshly shucked Gulf Coast oysters, with 1 pint liquor reserved

6 bacon slices, coarsely chopped

1 cup coarsely chopped yellow onion

½ cup coarsely chopped celery ribs

1 cup coarsely chopped button or oyster mushrooms

1 teaspoon minced garlic

¼ cup dry sherry

8 tablespoons (1 stick) unsalted butter, melted

5 tablespoons all-purpose flour

3 cups milk

3 sprigs fresh thyme

2 bay leaves

8-ounce brie cheese wheel, cut into 1-inch cubes (including rind)

Remaining trim from brie used for the croutons, cut into 1-inch cubes

Kosher salt

Freshly ground white pepper

FOR SERVING

1 stalk green onion, small chopped

FOR BRIE CROUTON: Preheat the oven to 350°F. Place rack in the center of the oven. Place sliced bread on baking pan. Bake until the bread is crisp and lightly browned, about 10 minutes. Remove from the oven and set aside to cool. Top the croutons with the thick slices of brie that should be long enough to cover each crouton; press firmly to adhere to each crouton. Place croutons on the tray in refrigerator until needed.

FOR SOUP: Strain the oysters and reserve the liquor until needed. Place a heavy-bottomed soup pot over medium heat. Add bacon, onion, and celery and stir frequently with a wooden spoon over low heat for about 2 to 3 minutes or until vegetables are slightly tender and bacon begins to lightly brown. Add the mushrooms, garlic, and sherry, and cook 2 more minutes. Add the melted butter and stir until you've created a smooth paste. Sprinkle the flour over the mixture; continue to stir for an additional 3 minutes over low heat, but do not brown the mixture.

Switch over to a wire whisk and stir in the oyster liquor and milk. Add thyme sprigs and bay leaves. Bring to a boil over medium-high heat, and then immediately reduce heat to a gentle simmer. Add the cubed brie, including the outer white flora rind, to soup. Continue to simmer until all the cheese has melted, about 30 minutes. Press the flora firmly against a slotted spoon to extract all the cheese. Lift out the brie flora and discard. Just before serving the soup, add oysters and cook for 3 to 4 minutes, or until edges curl and oysters are firm. Taste; adjust seasoning with salt and pepper to your liking.

TO ASSEMBLE: Position a rack 6 inches from the broiler and heat the broiler to medium-high.

Use a ladle to divide the soup into onion soup crocks, and then top each soup with a brie crouton for melting. Place under broiler for 2 to 3 minutes, until cheese melts and begins to turn golden on the edges. Sprinkle chopped green onion over each bowl. Serve right away.

Note: If you don't have enough oyster liquor, add clam juice or water to reach the correct amount.

OYSTER & ANDOUILLE GUMBO

—— 6 servings ——

Gumbo is the quintessential melting pot stew. It was made famous in New Orleans many crescent moons ago. Creole and Cajun dishes such as gumbo (of many types) were born in this part of the New World. This Louisiana Bayou style of cooking spread rapidly throughout the Deep South over the past several decades to neighboring cities such as Mobile and Pensacola. Historic Pensacola became something of an ethnic melting pot as its population grew. All along the northern Gulf of Mexico, the foodways of Spain, Mexico, Britain, American Indians, West Indies, Africa, and America melded to create the extraordinary richness and flavors of the Southern coastal cuisine we enjoy today. If you're fortunate enough to live along the Gulf of Mexico, easily available fresh bay shrimp and blue crab make excellent additions to this gumbo.

2 pints freshly shucked Gulf Coast oysters, with 3 pints liquor reserved

½ cup peanut or vegetable oil

¾ cup all-purpose flour

2 cups ½-inch-thick sliced andouille sausage

1 cup small-chopped yellow onion

1 cup small-chopped celery rib

1 cup small-chopped green pepper

1 tablespoon minced garlic

1 tomato, seeded and coarsely chopped

¼ pound thinly sliced fresh okra (optional)

2 bay leaves

1 teaspoon Creole seasoning

2 tablespoons Worcestershire sauce

Hot sauce

Kosher salt

Freshly ground black pepper

2 cups cooked white rice

1 cup small-chopped green onions

Strain the oysters and reserve the liquor until needed. Place a medium-size Dutch oven or heavy-bottomed soup pot over medium heat and add the oil. When oil begins to shimmer, about 4 minutes, whisk in the flour and stir constantly without stopping until a rich-colored dark brown roux is achieved, about 8 to 10 minutes. At about the 5-minute mark, the roux will look like caramel. The roux turns dark chocolate brown during the last minute of cooking. Be careful not to splash. Add the sausage, onion, celery, bell pepper, and garlic and stir in to cool down the roux. Stir until the vegetables are soft, about 4 minutes. Add the tomato, okra (if using), oyster liquor, bay leaves, and Creole seasoning. Whisk until well blended and smooth. Bring the gumbo to a boil, stirring frequently. Reduce heat to low and gently simmer for 30 minutes. Add Worcestershire and hot sauces. Just before serving, add oysters and cook until edges curl and oysters are firm, about 2 to 3 minutes. Taste; adjust seasoning with hot sauce, salt, and pepper. Serve in hot bowls over white rice, and top with green onions.

Note: If you don't have enough oyster liquor, add clam juice or water to reach the correct amount.

DARK OYSTER STEW
with BOUDIN BALLS

——— *6 servings* ———

Traditional French blood sausage, known as *boudin,* is produced in southern Louisiana, and consists of three essential ingredients—pork and pork liver, rice, and seasoning. Boudin has nearly as many variations as chaurice, the Creole and Cajun version of Spanish chorizo, also crafted in Louisiana. There are a seemingly endless number of recipe variations that have been adapted and modified by cooks and families alike. Boudin can be made by using different types of rice, substituting crawfish for white meat and game for dark meat, changing the blending ratios, selecting different sausage casings, and by fine-tuning seasonings to individuals' preferences. Some of my favorite oyster recipes combine oysters and spicy pork boudin, and this is one of them.

BOUDIN BALLS

1 pound authentic spicy boudin, casing removed

1 egg, lightly beaten

⅓ cup seasoned Italian bread crumbs

½ cup peanut oil

¼ cup all-purpose flour

SOUP

2 pints freshly shucked Gulf Coast oysters, with 3 pints liquor reserved

½ cup peanut oil

¾ cup all-purpose flour

1 cup small-chopped yellow onion

1 cup small-chopped celery rib

1 cup small-chopped green pepper

2 teaspoons minced garlic

Kosher salt

Freshly ground black pepper

FOR SERVING

1 cup small-chopped green onions

Hot sauce

FOR BOUDIN BALLS: Combine boudin, egg, and Italian bread crumbs in a small mixing bowl. Let meatball mixture rest for 30 minutes in the refrigerator before portioning. Use a 1-ounce ice cream scoop to portion the boudin mixture. Roll the portioned boudin mixture in your hands to form balls. Place them on a plate in the refrigerator until cooking.

Preheat a heavy skillet over medium-high heat with the oil. Lightly dust the boudin balls with flour and drop them one at a time into the hot oil. Fry until lightly browned all over, about 3 minutes. Use a slotted spoon to remove meatballs from the oil. Drain on a paper towel–lined plate until needed.

FOR SOUP: Strain oysters and reserve liquor until needed. Place a Dutch oven or heavy-bottomed soup pot over medium heat and add the oil. When oil begins to

shimmer, about 4 minutes, whisk in the flour and stir constantly without stopping until a rich-colored dark brown roux is achieved, about 8 to 10 minutes. At about the 5-minute mark, the roux will look like caramel. In the last minute of cooking, the roux will turn dark chocolate brown in color. Be careful not to splash; while continuing to stir, add the onion, celery, bell pepper, and garlic to cool down the roux. Stir until the vegetables are soft, about 4 minutes. Add oyster liquor, and whisk together to make a gumbolike, smooth stew. Reduce heat to low and simmer 20 minutes, stirring occasionally. Add the boudin balls and simmer an additional 7 minutes.

TO SERVE: Just before serving, add the oysters and cook 3 to 4 minutes or until they become firm and their edges have curled. Taste; adjust seasoning with salt and pepper. Divide the oysters, boudin balls, and stew into warm soup bowls. Garnish with green onions, and serve right away with hot sauce.

Note: If you don't have enough oyster liquor, add clam juice or water to reach the correct amount.

Oyster Farm
APALACHICOLA
FLORIDA

This is a profile on a special oyster-farming area instead of just a single farm. Apalachicola remains one of the more remote Old Florida cities along the Gulf of Mexico. It is in the heart of Florida's hurricane alley, a.k.a. "Forgotten Coast," which is a regional name used to designate the relatively undeveloped, quiet section of the Panhandle's "Big Bend" coastline stretching from Mexico Beach to Apalachee Bay. It's one of my favorite places to visit and spend the night along the Gulf of Mexico. A trip to this area is as good as it gets, especially for getting away from it all.

The Forgotten Coast is known for its pristine bays, sugar-white beaches, coastal marshlands, and estuaries, which are rich with sea life. Apalachicola Bay was once widely recognized for its contributing bottom-oyster culture production for the state, but not so much anymore. Oyster fishermen there still use tongs to harvest oysters the old-fashioned way. Apalachicola Bay includes St. George Sound, East Bay, Apalachicola Bay, St. Vincent Sound, and Indian Lagoon, along with their respective canals, rivers, and creeks. Today, the once-vibrant oyster industry is managing to show renewed, healthy signs of life in Apalachicola Bay via a few oystermen and oyster women who work the waters and are harvesting one or two bags each day.

Government agencies have stepped in to prevent the decimation of the Apalachicola oyster by initiating bay closures and managing new handling and harvesting procedures that prevent improper handling and over-harvesting, providing adequate time for juvenile oyster growth. In Apalachicola, the dormant oyster industry manages to stay focused on replanting oyster beds as best they can while local and state agencies provide constant water testing.

Natural oyster reefs aren't spawning as plentifully as in the past and the harvests are in decline, yet shellfish consumption is at an all-time high and good oysters are in vogue. When Apalachicola does bounce back, there might be a bounty of oysters hitting the market again someday soon. Oyster optimism at its finest!

Tommy Ward and his family have been in business in Apalachicola for three generations under the name of 13 Mile Brand seafood. The name comes from the location of the family's seafood facility, which is located 13 miles west of Apalachicola. The family operates an oyster-processing facility at 13 Mile and runs a shrimp

A burnt yellow sunset against the oyster pile located at Buddy Ward and Sons Seafood at 13 Mile Road along Apalachicola Bay.

Oyster boat and tongs at East Point boat launch, just east of Apalachicola's John Gorrie Memorial bridge (above). An Alligator Harbor farm-raised oyster from Playing Hooky owner and oyster farmer Sharon Fitzgerald (right).

facility/retail market in the town. They also maintain some of the oldest granted underwater leases for bottom-oyster harvesting in the western end of Apalachicola Bay. True to the family's custodian attitude for the bay, they have been adding their processed and discarded oyster shells back to the bay for many years as a rebuilding program for oyster habitats. Spat (baby oysters) can attach and grow on the shells, and this helps to repopulate their numbers.

To get the word out about the state of bottom-culture oyster farming for Apalachicola, I have worked closely with the Ward family by leading oyster-focused events like Outstanding in the Field (a California-based farm-to-table, roving, culinary adventure) in 2014, 2015, and 2016.

In 2015, Tommy and his family of prominent oyster-reef farmers first introduced me to farm-raised, cage-grown oysters from Alligator Harbor. I was blown away.

It was the first time I tasted an off-bottom–farmed oyster raised by Sharon Fitzgerald of Playing Hooky, who often supplies pristine, farm-raised singles to 13 Mile Seafood Market. Fitzgerald, a family clam grower, produces oysters that are briny and meaty. Franklin County, home to Alligator Harbor, currently has only two oyster aquaculture leases, which are located near Teresa Beach. In 2017, TJ Ward purchased ranching equipment for growing oysters in Indian Lagoon: the only aquaculture lease for Gulf County.

APALACHICOLA OYSTER STEW

—— 6 servings ——

In Apalachicola, bottomland oystermen learned how and when to harvest oysters the old-fashioned way. It takes about two days of west wind to "salt up" oysters, as briny waters from the Gulf of Mexico blow in through Indian Pass. The saying goes, "if you like salty oysters, and you're in Apalachicola, lick a finger, stick it in the air, and head for a restaurant that gets its oysters from the side of the bay the wind is coming from." The cooks around the Apalachicola area like to keep their oyster stew recipes simple. Here's my spruced-up version for preparing their namesake bay oyster stew, from a remote and historic Florida coastal town once famous for timber, cotton, sponges, seafood, and one of the tastiest oysters in the world.

2 pints freshly shucked Gulf Coast oysters, with 1 cup liquor reserved

1 tablespoon pure olive oil

¼ pound (12 slices) thick-sliced smoky pork sausage

1 cup small-chopped yellow onion

1 celery rib, small chopped

1 tablespoon minced garlic

1 cup peeled and small-chopped russet potatoes

1 sprig fresh thyme

½ cup dry white wine

Kosher salt

White pepper

1 cup heavy cream

1 bay leaf

1 cup milk

Hot sauce

½ cup small-chopped green onions, white and light green parts only

Strain oysters and reserve the liquor until needed. Place a medium Dutch oven or heavy-bottomed soup pot over medium heat and add the oil. Heat oil for 2 minutes, then add the sausage and stir until cooked, about 3 minutes. Add the onion, celery, garlic, potatoes, and thyme; stir occasionally for 5 minutes to soften the vegetables. Add the wine and stir well. Lightly season the vegetables with salt and pepper. Reduce the heat to medium-low; add oyster liquor, heavy cream, and bay leaf. Bring to a boil, and then immediately reduce heat to a low simmer and cook for 20 minutes, or until the potatoes are tender. Just before serving, add the oysters and milk to the stew. Cook for 5 to 7 minutes or until oysters become firm and edges curl. Remove thyme stem and bay leaf. Taste; adjust seasoning with salt and pepper. Ladle into bowls and serve with hot sauce and green onions.

Note: *If you don't have enough oyster liquor, add clam juice or water to reach the correct amount.*

OYSTER STEW

with GOCHUJANG & COCONUT CREAM

6 servings

During the mid-1980s, many Vietnamese found a second home along the coastlines of Florida, Alabama, Mississippi, and Louisiana. Many brought their fishing experience with them. They used fishing, fish cutting, bottomland oystering, oyster processing, and shrimping as ways to support their families. Early on, I discovered that one of my favorite ways to prepare oyster stew is with coconut cream and Far East flavors. This stew broth is rather light and delicate, ever-so-slightly thickened with flour, and elegantly rich. I have adapted this recipe to include the Korean hot pepper paste gochujang, which can be found at most Korean and Asian markets.

2 pints freshly shucked Gulf Coast oysters, with 3 cups liquor reserved

6 tablespoons (¾ stick) unsalted butter

1 cup small-chopped green onions, greens reserved for garnish

3 tablespoons minced lemongrass

1 tablespoon minced garlic

1 tablespoon grated fresh gingerroot

¼ cup mirin (sweet rice wine)

4 tablespoons rice flour

3 cups coconut milk or cream

2 tablespoons fish sauce

2 tablespoons soy sauce

1 tablespoon gochujang paste

4 tablespoons miso paste

1 Thai chili, minced

2 tablespoons coarsely chopped cilantro

Kosher salt

Freshly ground black pepper

Strain oysters and reserve the liquor until needed. Melt the butter in a heavy-bottomed soup pot over medium heat. Add the white part of the green onions, lemongrass, garlic, and ginger; stir to coat with butter. Add the mirin and stir to cook for 2 minutes. Sprinkle the flour over the mixture and cook on low heat for 5 minutes, stirring frequently and until flour has disappeared. Add coconut milk, oyster liquor, fish sauce, and soy sauce. Increase heat and bring to a boil until slightly thickened, about 5 minutes. Reduce heat to a gentle simmer and then add gochujang, miso, and chili. Stir and simmer for 15 minutes. Just before serving, add the oysters and cilantro and simmer until oysters are firm and edges begin to curl, about 2 to 3 minutes. Remove from heat. Taste; adjust seasoning with salt and pepper. Ladle soup into hot bowls and garnish with green parts of green onion. Serve right away.

Note: If you don't have enough oyster liquor, add clam juice or water to reach the correct amount.

STOUT & SMOKED CHEDDAR SOUP
with FRIED OYSTERS

———— 6 servings ————

The truly great cooks have a vision for their dishes. After selecting winning ingredients, they have the knowledge and experience to draw upon to marry them with just the right flavors to produce memorable results. Whether it is as simple as combining onions and garlic, adding jalapeño pepper to a relish, or just serving saltine crackers with oysters, some food pairings simply don't need to be gussied up. This soup is one of those, and that's what folks adore. Just imagine sipping on a simple, velvety soup, flavored with a stout beer, smoky cheese, and crispy fried oysters. I'm salivating just thinking about the last time I made it.

8 tablespoons (1 stick) unsalted butter

½ pound small-chopped country or smoked ham

1 cup small-chopped yellow onion

½ cup small-chopped celery rib

2 tablespoons minced garlic

6 tablespoons all-purpose flour

1 cup chicken broth

3 cups half-and-half

1 medium russet potato, peeled and small chopped

3 tablespoons Worcestershire sauce

3 tablespoons hot sauce (Louisiana brand preferred)

1 12-ounce bottle craft stout beer

1½ pounds smoked cheddar cheese, grated

Kosher salt

Freshly ground white pepper

12 or more fried Gulf Coast oysters (see Simple Fried Oysters recipe on page 98)

3 green onions (both white and light greens), small chopped

Melt the butter in a heavy-bottomed soup pot over medium heat. Add the ham, onion, and celery. Stir and cook for 5 minutes or until onions become tender, and then stir in garlic. Sprinkle in flour and use a wooden spoon to mix in completely. Continue to stir the mixture for 5 minutes. Add chicken broth, stir, and bring mixture to a boil. Add half-and-half, potatoes, Worcestershire sauce, hot sauce, and beer; adjust heat to medium-low and simmer for 20 minutes, or until potatoes are tender. Stir in cheese and whisk to blend. Serve unstrained or for a velvety-smooth texture, place in blender and run on low speed for 30 seconds. Taste; adjust seasoning with salt and pepper. Divide into individual hot soup bowls and top each portion with two or more fried oysters and pinch of green onions. Serve right away.

DIRTY OYSTER ROCKEFELLER SOUP

6 servings

Oysters Rockefeller was created at historic Antoine's Restaurant in 1899 in New Orleans, Louisiana, about 200 miles from Pensacola. The oyster preparation has become a culinary tradition all along the coastal states of the Gulf of Mexico and around the country. Of course, there are many versions of the Rockefeller oyster preparation in a shell, and equally as many oyster soup concoctions found in a bowl. Throwing in a bit of meat is not the traditional way of making the soup, but adding sausage or ground pork livers to the recipe is a delicious reason to make it dirty. That's how my Dirty Oyster Rockefeller Soup was born.

1 pound fresh baby spinach leaves, rinsed	1 small onion, coarsely chopped
2 pints Gulf Coast oysters, freshly shucked and 1 cup liquor reserved	6 tablespoons all-purpose flour
	5 cloves garlic, minced
½ pound ground chaurice or andouille sausage	3 cups half-and-half
	Kosher salt
2–3 ounces anise-flavored liqueur (such as Pernod, Herbsaint, or Ouzo)	Pinch cayenne pepper
	Small wedge aged Parmigiano Reggiano

Steam spinach to wilt, about 2 minutes. Place in a strainer and squeeze to remove liquid. Place cooked spinach on a cutting surface and rough chop. Set aside until needed.

Strain oysters and reserve the liquor until needed. Place a medium Dutch oven over medium-high heat. Remove the sausage from its casing, add to the pan, and break it up with a flat-tip spatula until cooked, about 7 minutes. Add the anise-flavored liqueur and simmer for 3 minutes. Add the onion and stir until soft, about 5 minutes. Sprinkle in the flour and stir to blend in completely; cook for 3 to 4 minutes. Add the garlic, oyster liquor, half-and-half, and stir well. Increase heat to medium and stir frequently until slightly thickened, about 20 minutes.

Just before serving, add the chopped spinach and oysters. Increase heat to medium-high and stir occasionally until oysters become firm and edges curl, about 5 minutes. Taste; adjust seasoning with salt and cayenne pepper. Grate fresh parmesan over top. Serve right away.

Note: If you don't have enough oyster liquor, add clam juice or water to reach the correct amount.

104

110

112

122

CHAPTER 5

PAN & DEEP FRIED

SIMPLE FRIED OYSTERS

6 servings

Preparing superb-tasting oysters starts with a reputable seafood supplier who you can rely on to properly handle processed, freshly shucked oysters or shell oysters from the Gulf of Mexico. For sustainably harvested oysters and shrimp, I can trust Chris Nelson of Bon Secour Fisheries, Inc. in Alabama. For oysters, shrimp, fresh fish, and crab, I can trust my longtime friend Ray Boyer of Maria's Fresh Seafood Market in Pensacola to source from the Gulf's best oyster and crab processors, shrimpers, and fishermen. See the resource section to find Bon Secour and Maria's.

2 sleeves (100) saltine crackers

½ cup all-purpose flour

1 teaspoon freshly ground black pepper

24 Gulf Coast oysters in their shells (see note) or 2 pints freshly shucked

3 cups vegetable or peanut oil

Kosher salt

Lemon wedges

Place crackers in food processor with a knife blade; pulse to make medium-fine crumbs, and then transfer into a medium bowl. Add flour and pepper. Strain the oysters and then drop them into the cracker mixture a few at a time, keeping them separated. Place them on a platter in a single layer. Sprinkle few pinches of the flour mixture over top of the coated oysters. Repeat until all the oysters have been used. Place in refrigerator until frying. Just before frying, tap off any excess flour mixture.

Heat frying oil to 350°F in a deep skillet using a clip-on thermometer and fry the coated oysters in two batches, for 2 to 3 minutes (depending on their size) or until golden brown. Place them on a paper towel–lined plate and sprinkle with salt. Using your favorite oyster platter, stack the fried oysters, add lemon wedges, and serve right away.

Note: If using shelled oysters, scrub and rinse the shell oysters well to remove any debris. Shuck the oysters and reserve them in their liquor. Place the oysters and liquor in a small bowl and refrigerate them until ready to use. Reserve the bottom cupped shells. Place the bottom shells in a large sauce pot, submerge the shells in water, place the pot over medium-high heat, and boil for 5 minutes. Remove from water and let cool on a kitchen towel or wire rack.

CHICKEN-FRIED OYSTERS

—— 6 servings ——

Country, or chicken-fried, proteins, such as beef, fish, and oysters, begin with a coating of seasoned flour, followed by a dip in egg and milk wash, and then another coating of the seasoned flour. It's that simple. Double-coated! I love the simplicity of crispy-frying the thick-coated oysters, and then making a gravy by using a few tablespoons of the frying fat right in the same skillet. Decades ago, I often felt that I wouldn't make much of a Southerner, but this classic Southern cooking method has made me feel like I was born to be one.

OYSTERS

2 eggs, lightly beaten

2 cups milk

2 cups all-purpose flour

2 teaspoons Old Bay seasoning

1 teaspoon freshly ground black pepper

¼ teaspoon cayenne pepper

24 Gulf Coast oysters (see note on page 99) or 2 pints freshly shucked oysters, 4 tablespoons liquor reserved for gravy

3 cups vegetable or peanut oil

Kosher salt

GRAVY

4 tablespoons oil reserved from frying

4 tablespoons all-purpose flour

1½ cups half-and-half

4 tablespoons reserved oyster liquor

Kosher salt

Freshly ground black pepper

FOR OYSTERS: Whisk the eggs and milk together in a medium bowl. Mix the flour, Old Bay seasoning, black pepper, and cayenne in a second medium bowl. Place the shucked oysters in a third medium bowl. Coat the oysters, a few at a time, in the seasoned flour mixture. Place the oysters into the egg wash and submerge to coat completely. Last, use a fork to place them back into the seasoned flour mixture and coat a second time. Lay them on a cookie pan in a single layer, then repeat with the remaining oysters.

TO FRY: Heat the oil in a medium Dutch oven or a large heavy skillet over medium heat for 5 minutes. The oil is ready for frying if you add a pinch of flour and it sizzles and then turns brown. Add half the coated oysters a few at a time; cook for 2 to 3 minutes on each side (depending on their size), or until golden brown, turning once. Use a slotted spoon to lift the fried oysters from the oil and place onto a paper towel–lined plate to drain. Repeat until all the oysters have been fried. Season with salt.

FOR GRAVY: After all the oysters have been fried, strain the frying oil into a heatproof bowl. Reserve 4 tablespoons of oil and discard the rest. Use a paper towel to wipe the pan and remove any burnt bits. Return skillet to the stove over medium-low heat. Add reserved frying oil to the skillet and allow it to heat up. Sprinkle flour evenly over the oil. Whisk, mixing the flour with the oil (you're making a roux). Keep cooking until the roux reaches a pale white color, about 3 minutes. Pour in the half-and-half and oyster liquor, whisking constantly until smooth. Taste; adjust seasoning with salt and pepper.

TO SERVE: Arrange the oyster shells on a platter. Place 1 teaspoon of gravy in the center of each shell, and then top with 1 fried oyster. Repeat until all the shells have been filled. If not using shells, use your favorite oyster platter, stack the fried oysters, and serve gravy in a dipping bowl. Serve right away.

TEMPURA FRIED OYSTERS
with HOT & SWEET DIPPING SAUCE

6 servings; sauce makes about 2 cups

I'm pushing the tempura envelope with this recipe. Southern Japan is credited for this century-old cooking preparation. From shrimp to thin strips of vegetables, foods are dipped into a chilled pancakelike batter and then flash-fried using slightly hotter oil than a typical deep-fry. I love the added texture of medium-ground cornmeal, the added flavor of fine-ground corn flour, and the taste of malty beer replacing soda water for my recipe. Typically, you won't find oysters prepared this way. There's no soy sauce or Asian flavors of any kind in this recipe, just thin-batter–crusted oysters with my hot and sweet dipping sauce.

HOT & SWEET DIPPING SAUCE

- 10 ounces peach or apricot preserves
- 4 tablespoons sherry vinegar
- ¼ cup Chardonnay
- 2 tablespoons hot sauce
- 1 jalapeño pepper, seeded and minced
- 2 tablespoons minced shallot
- 1 teaspoon red pepper flakes
- Kosher salt

TEMPURA FRIED OYSTERS

- ½ cup corn flour
- ½ cup cornmeal
- 1 cup rice flour
- 1 teaspoon baking powder
- 1 12-ounce beer
- 3 cups vegetable oil for frying
- 24 Gulf Coast oysters in their shells (see note on page 99) or 2 pints freshly shucked
- Pinch fine sea salt

FOR HOT & SWEET DIPPING SAUCE: Combine the preserves, vinegar, wine, hot sauce, jalapeño, shallot, and red pepper flakes in a small sauce pot; stir and bring to a boil. Reduce heat and simmer for 5 minutes. Taste; adjust seasoning with salt.

FOR TEMPURA FRIED OYSTERS: Combine corn flour, cornmeal, rice flour, and baking powder in a medium bowl. Make a well in the center, stir in beer, and mix ingredients from the center out. Blend until batter is smooth like pancake batter. Place in an airtight container in the refrigerator to chill down completely before using, about 1 hour.

TO FRY: Heat oil to 350°F in a medium Dutch oven or large heavy skillet with a clip-on thermometer. Lightly season the oysters with a pinch of sea salt, and then use a toothpick or wooden skewer to spear the oyster and cover completely in the batter. Place them one by one directly into the hot oil and let them fall from the toothpick. Fry a few at a time for 1 to 2 minutes (depending on their size), until golden brown. Turn once for even color. Use a slotted spoon to lift them from the oil and place them on a paper towel–lined plate. Repeat until all the oysters have been used.

TO SERVE: Arrange the oyster shells face up on a platter. Place one fried oyster in each shell. Repeat until all the shells have been filled. Spoon dipping sauce over each oyster and serve right away. If not using shells, use your favorite oyster platter, stack the tempura fried oysters, and serve right away with a bowl of dipping sauce.

Oyster Farm
GRAND ISLE SEA FARM
LOUISIANA

In 2012, Marcos Guerrero was one of the first to apply for a license to grow oysters in the Gulf of Mexico around Caminada Bay when the Louisiana Aquaculture Park was created. This pristine location allows the winds and vital nutrients to flow easily through the pass, creating an estuary suitable for maximizing oyster growth. For Guerrero, hatchery to harvest of a market-size 3-inch oyster requires about 12 months. He and his family (originally from South America and Italy) are involved with the operation: his wife, Lali; daughter, Natalia; and sons, Aldo and Boris. While touring Grand Isle, I met Boris and his wife at the Grand Isle marina.

Gulf Coast off-bottom farming trends, on-farm larvae, and seed nurseries are popping up throughout the Gulf states. Triple N Oyster Farm in Louisiana, Navy Cove Oyster Company in Alabama, and Pensacola Bay Oyster Company in Florida are a few examples of others making the addition to their farms. Marcos says, "By undertaking to run our own nursery, we increase our independence and involvement in the process of oyster farming. It allows us to take part in growing oysters from the very beginning to the end." Since my visit to Grand Isle, Marcos is also hatching larvae and producing his own oyster seeds: the growing trend!

OYSTERS & BACON

4 servings

Angels on horseback is traditionally a hot hors d'oeuvre of plump oysters wrapped with strips of bacon, then skewered and baked. They became popular in the 19th century and have remained a classic. The dish is decadent and delicious. And there's just something pure and simple about the duo that is the inspiration behind recreating what I simply call Oysters & Bacon. These heavenly crispy little angels are paired with molasses, brown sugar, spicy aioli, and salt-cured pork belly that I smoke with pecan wood until dark and intensely smoke-flavored; you can use any strongly smoked bacon, though. Now I'm salivating!

SPICY AIOLI

2 egg yolks

1 tablespoon minced garlic

1 teaspoon minced shallot

1 tablespoon fresh lime juice

½ teaspoon smoky paprika

½ teaspoon crushed red pepper flakes

1½ cups olive oil

1 tablespoon tepid water

Kosher salt

Freshly ground black pepper

BACON

6 ¼-inch thick slices heavily cured and smoked slab bacon (such as Bill-E's Small Batch Bacon)

OYSTERS

1 stalk green onion

1 cup cornmeal

1 cup corn flour

2 teaspoons kosher salt

½ teaspoon cayenne pepper

2 pints freshly shucked Gulf Coast oysters

3 cups vegetable or peanut oil

FOR SPICY AIOLI: In a food processor with a knife blade, combine the egg yolks, garlic, shallot, lime juice, paprika, and red pepper flakes; pulse to process. With the machine running, slowly drizzle in oil until all has been used. Aioli mixture should be creamy and thick. Adjust sauce consistency with water until smooth like thick mayonnaise. Taste, and seasoning with salt and pepper to your liking.

FOR BACON: Preheat a large heavy skillet or griddle to medium high. Place the bacon slices flat, leaving ½-inch or more between slices. Use a foil-wrapped brick as a weight to flatten and speed up browning of the bacon. Cook and brown for 2 to 3 minutes on each side, and then place onto a paper towel–lined plate to drain. Slice the bacon into 1-inch lengths.

FOR OYSTERS: Cut the green onions into long match sticks and soak in ice water for 2 hours, or until they curl. Mix together cornmeal, corn flour, salt, and

cayenne pepper in a medium bowl. Strain the oysters and reserve liquor in a sealed container in the freezer for future use. Coat the oysters in the corn flour mixture a few at a time, keeping them separated. Place them on a platter in a single layer. Sprinkle a few pinches of the cornmeal mixture over top of the coated oysters. Repeat with remaining oysters. Just before frying, tap off any excess cornmeal mixture.

TO FRY: Heat the oil in a Dutch oven or large heavy skillet over medium heat for 4 to 5 minutes; there should only be about 1 inch of oil in the pan. The oil is ready for frying if you add a pinch of corn flour and it sizzles and oil is shimmering. Add half the coated oysters a few at a time, and fry 2 or 3 minutes (depending on their size), until golden brown. Use a slotted spoon to lift the fried oysters from the oil; place onto a paper towel–lined plate to drain. Repeat until all the oysters are fried.

TO ASSEMBLE: Place bacon slices onto a platter with enough space between so they do not touch. Top bacon with one fried oyster, and then a dab of spicy aioli. Garnish with a green onion curl on top of each. Serve right away.

PAN-FRIED OYSTERS
& SMOKED PORK BELLY

—— 6 servings ——

It was culinary nirvana the very first time I cooked at the James Beard House in 1993. I learned how to prepare pan-fried oysters with cornmeal coating, which is a notable Edna Lewis recipe. I cooked alongside Scott Peacock as we prepared dinner for Edna Lewis's 77th birthday celebration. This was a special event indeed. We prepared an array of her favorite recipes. Of course, for biscuits and fried chicken, the two chefs would always render pork fat for their lard. I fashioned this recipe in honor of those incredible pan-fried oysters cooked the same way, but this time I rendered them in smoky lard and served them with a pile of crispy pork belly.

RENDERED PORK BELLY

1 pound cured and smoked pork belly (unsliced bacon)

1 pound natural lard

OYSTERS

24 Gulf Coast oysters in their shells (see note on page 99) or 2 pints freshly shucked

4 eggs, well beaten

1½ cups saltine cracker meal (see Simple Fried Oysters recipe on page 98)

½ cup all-purpose flour

Pinch kosher salt

½ teaspoon freshly ground black pepper

8 tablespoons (1 stick) unsalted butter

FOR RENDERED PORK BELLY: Cut the smoked bacon into ¾-inch pieces. Combine the bacon pieces and lard in a medium Dutch oven or large heavy skillet over medium-low heat. The lard will help cook the bacon without sticking to the pan. The rendering will cause the bacon to float, and when crispy it can easily be removed with a slotted spoon, about 30 minutes. Remove the bacon onto a paper towel–lined plate to drain. Strain the lard into an ovenproof bowl. Wipe the skillet with a paper towel to remove any burned bits.

FOR OYSTERS: Place beaten eggs in a medium bowl. Mix together the cracker meal, flour, salt, and pepper in a shallow dish. Strain the oysters and then drop them into the beaten egg; stir to coat well. Use a fork to lift out each oyster; coat in the cracker meal mixture a few at a time, keeping them separated. Place them on a platter in a single layer. Sprinkle a few pinches of the cracker meal mixture over top of the coated oysters. Repeat until all the oysters have been coated. Just before frying, tap off any excess cracker meal mixture.

TO FRY: Heat half the butter and half the rendered lard over medium heat for 3 to 4 minutes. The lard mixture is ready for frying once you add a pinch of cracker meal mixture and it sizzles and turns brown. Fry the coated oysters a few at a time for 2 to 3 minutes, until golden brown. Fry in two batches, or until all the coated oysters have been used. Place them on a paper towel–lined plate to drain.

TO SERVE: Place the oysters on a platter and pile high, along with the crispy pork belly.

CORNMEAL-COATED OYSTERS
with **CRISPY BACON**

4 servings

Few cooking memories evoke more happiness for me than preparing stone-ground grits, fried chicken, cornmeal-crusted oysters, collard greens, buttermilk biscuits, and slaw with the remarkable 76-year-old chef Edna Lewis and the young, emphatic chef Scott Peacock. I picked up many recipe tricks from them along the way. One of them was adding smoky bacon to the skillet fat when frying chicken, which I modified for pan-frying oysters. Of course, the crispy bacon slices try their best to make it to the paper towel for draining, but they are hard to resist in the moment.

1 cup cornmeal

1 cup corn flour

2 teaspoons kosher salt

½ teaspoon cayenne pepper

2 pints freshly shucked Gulf
   Coast oysters

8 strips smoky bacon

3 cups vegetable or peanut oil

Lemon wedges

Mix together cornmeal, corn flour, salt, and cayenne pepper in a medium bowl. Strain the oysters and reserve liquor in a sealed container in the freezer for future use. Coat the oysters in the corn flour mixture a few at a time, keeping them separated. Place them on a platter in a single layer. Sprinkle a few pinches of the cornmeal mixture over top of the coated oysters. Repeat with remaining oysters. Just before frying, tap off any excess cornmeal mixture.

Heat the oil in Dutch oven or large heavy skillet. Allow 1 inch of shallow frying oil for the pan, and place over medium heat for 4 to 5 minutes. The oil is ready for frying if you add a pinch of corn flour and it sizzles and oil is shimmering. Add four strips of bacon to the frying oil, and let cook halfway, about 1 minute. Add half the coated oysters a few at a time, and fry 2 or 3 minutes (depending on their size), until golden brown. Use a slotted spoon to lift the fried oysters and crispy bacon from the oil, and place onto a paper towel–lined plate to drain. Repeat for second batch, using all the bacon and oysters. Add a pinch of salt and pile the bacon and oysters high. Serve right away with lemon wedges.

1821 CANNONBALL OYSTERS

6 servings

In Pensacola's Historic Downtown District rests Plaza Ferdinand, a landmark park where our seventh President of the United States (1829–1837), Andrew Jackson (General Jackson at the time), oversaw the transfer of Florida from Spain to the United States in 1821. Right across the street at Jackson's Steakhouse, I was visiting with my good friend and marksman "Cannonball Curtis" and created this simple oyster recipe for him. This is how the dish got the name "1821 Cannonball Oysters." Freshly shucked, bottom-harvested Gulf Coast oysters are ideal for this crispy fried preparation, and pair excellently with my Vietnamese-style sweet and spicy chili sauce.

SWEET & SPICY GARLIC CHILI SAUCE

- 4 tablespoons seasoned rice wine vinegar
- 3 tablespoons fish sauce
- 3 tablespoons fresh lemon juice
- 1 tablespoon grated fresh ginger
- 3 tablespoons garlic chili paste
- 2 tablespoons finely chopped cilantro
- ¾ cup light corn syrup

OYSTERS

- 1 egg, lightly beaten
- 1 cup milk
- 2 cups all-purpose flour
- 2 teaspoons kosher salt
- 1 teaspoon ground black pepper
- 3 cups finely ground panko breadcrumbs
- 24 Gulf Coast oysters in their liquor (see note on page 99) or 2 pints freshly shucked oysters
- 3 cups vegetable or peanut oil

FOR SWEET & SPICY GARLIC CHILI SAUCE: Combine all ingredients in a small sauce pot. Whisk together over low heat, about 3 minutes. Remove from heat, pour into small bowl, and allow the sauce to cool down completely. Sauce can be made a few days in advance and stored in an airtight container in refrigerator.

FOR OYSTERS: Whisk the egg and milk (egg wash) in a mixing bowl and blend well. Mix the flour, salt, and pepper in a shallow mixing bowl. Place the breadcrumbs in a third mixing bowl. Coat the oysters with seasoned flour, a few at a time, until evenly coated. Drop them into the egg wash, a few at a time, and submerge to coat well. Remove them from the egg wash and coat completely with panko breadcrumbs. Lay them on a cookie sheet in a single layer, and repeat until all the oysters have been used.

TO FRY: Heat the oil to 350°F, using a medium Dutch oven or large heavy skillet and a clip-on thermometer. Fry the breaded oysters a few at a time, for 2 or 3 minutes (depending on their size), until golden brown. Use a slotted spoon to lift the fried oysters from the oil and place on a paper towel–lined plate to drain. Fry in batches until finished.

TO SERVE: Arrange the oyster shells on a platter. Place one fried oyster in each shell and top with 1 tablespoon of sauce. Repeat until all the shells have been filled. If using fresh-shucked oysters in the pint container, use your favorite oyster platter for serving. Just before serving, toss the fried oysters in a large bowl with half the chili sauce, and pile them high on the platter. Pour remaining sauce into a sauce dish for dipping, and serve right away.

CRACKLING-CRUSTED OYSTERS
on DEVILED EGGS

6 servings

Making perfect cracklings, a.k.a. chicharrons, from scratch requires trimming fatback, drying pork skin, and liquefying fat for frying. This process involves a full day in the kitchen, which I am most accustomed too. However, I wanted folks to try this deviled egg recipe at home by only having to make one or two trips to the market and without all the fuss. Deviled eggs themselves are plenty time-consuming and finger-licking good, after all. Frying your oysters in this manner will be a heck of a lot quicker than making cracklings from scratch, and you'll get terrific results.

DEVILED EGGS

12 large eggs

5 tablespoons mayonnaise

3 tablespoons minced celery

2 tablespoons finely chopped shallots

2 teaspoons Creole mustard

2 tablespoons heavy cream

3 dashes your favorite hot sauce

Kosher salt

Freshly ground black pepper

CRACKLING-CRUSTED OYSTERS

24 freshly shucked Gulf Coast oysters

2 egg whites, lightly beaten

3 2½-ounce bags spicy fried pork rinds (see note)

½ cup rice flour

½ tablespoon Creole spice

Vegetable oil or lard, for frying

FOR DEVILED EGGS: Carefully place eggs in the bottom of a medium soup pot with water to cover, and then bring to a boil. Once water has reached a boil, reduce heat and set a timer to simmer for exactly 5 minutes. Turn off heat, cover pot, and set timer for another 5 minutes for a total of 10 minutes in the water. Drain off hot water, lift and shake the pan lightly to break the egg shells, and then transfer eggs to a bowl of ice water; let sit until cool enough to handle. Peel right away. Perfect eggs every time! Halve eggs lengthwise. Separate the boiled yolks into a small bowl and place the halved whites on a cookie sheet face up. Combine yolks, mayonnaise, celery, shallot, mustard, heavy cream, and hot sauce in a small bowl and gently mash. Taste; adjust seasoning with salt and pepper. Using two forks or a pastry bag with a star tip, fill egg halves with deviled egg mixture.

CRACKLING-CRUSTED OYSTERS
on DEVILED EGGS
—— *continued* ——

FOR CRACKLING-CRUSTED OYSTERS: Strain oysters into a medium bowl and cover them in the egg whites. Reserve the liquor in sealable containers or zip top bags, and place in the freezer for future use. In a food processor with a knife blade, add the fried pork rinds and pulse to grind fine. Mix the ground pork rinds, flour, and Creole spice in a medium bowl. Lift the oysters out of the egg whites, a few at a time, and coat them evenly with the ground pork rind mixture. Lift them out and tap off any excess. Set the coated oysters aside on a platter or cookie sheet, and continue coating the remaining oysters until all have been used.

TO FRY: Heat the frying oil to 350°F using a deep skillet and a clip-on thermometer. Deep-fry the breaded oysters a few at a time, for 2 or 3 minutes (depending on their size), until golden brown. Use a slotted spoon to lift the fried oysters from the oil and place onto a paper towel–lined plate to drain. Fry in small batches until finished.

TO SERVE: Top each deviled egg with a fried oyster and serve right away with hot sauce.

Note: Sourcing pork skin and making fried pork rinds from scratch is best; however, it's time-consuming and requires planning ahead. The second-best option is to locate dehydrated pork rind pellets and fry them yourself. The simplest option is to buy pork rinds already fried and seasoned, and ready to grind; but be aware, there are preservatives and often MSG added.

OYSTER FRY

with CORN RELISH & BLUE CHEESE

6 servings

Oysters are prized for regional preparations. Along the Gulf Coast, the most popular way to prepare oysters is to deep-fry them. It's easy, and they're delicious—especially when you buy them shucked and packed in their own liquor.

RELISH

5 tablespoons pure olive oil

4 or 5 ears fresh sweet corn, husk and silk removed

1 cup finely chopped red bell pepper

1 jalapeño pepper, seeded and finely chopped

¼ cup finely chopped red onion

2 tablespoons finely chopped parsley

½ cup good-quality blue cheese, broken

Kosher salt

Freshly ground black pepper

OYSTERS

2 pints freshly shucked Gulf Coast oysters

1 egg, lightly beaten

1 cup buttermilk

⅓ cup hot sauce

2 cups all-purpose flour

1 tablespoon Creole spice

3 cups panko breadcrumbs

3 cups vegetable or peanut oil

Lemon wedges

FOR RELISH: Preheat charcoal or gas grill to medium-high. Dip a paper towel in the oil and rub over the corn. Place corn on grill, turning every few minutes, until the ears are charred, about 10 minutes. Remove from grill and let cool. Cut off the stem ends so the corn stands upright on your cutting board. Slice straight down the sides to remove kernels. Mix corn kernels, pepper, jalapeño, onion, parsley, and blue cheese in a medium bowl. Taste the relish; adjust seasoning with salt and pepper. Set aside.

FOR OYSTERS: Strain the oysters. Reserve the liquor in sealable containers or zip top bags, and place in the freezer for future use. Mix egg, buttermilk, and hot sauce in a medium bowl. Mix flour and Creole spice in another bowl. Place panko in a third bowl or shallow dish. Coat the oysters in seasoned flour, a few at a time; dip in buttermilk mixture, use a fork to remove, and coat in bread crumbs. Repeat until all the oysters have been coated. Place on a platter or cookie sheet in a single layer.

TO FRY: Heat the frying oil to 350°F in a medium Dutch oven or large heavy skillet using a clip-on thermometer, and fry the breaded oysters in batches for 2 to 3 minutes, until golden brown. Tap to remove any excess breading before frying.

TO SERVE: Arrange on a platter and spoon relish over top. Serve right away with lemon wedges.

MURDER POINT OYSTER COMPANY
ALABAMA

Murder Point Oyster Company is second to none when it comes to Alabama off-bottom oyster farming. The story of Murder Point is a sinister one that gets your attention. Formerly known as Myrtle Point, this sliver of land along Portersville Bay witnessed a deadly dealing back in 1927 over a bottom-bed oyster lease. Hence, their tagline: "Oysters Worth Killing For." I had tasted Murder Point's oysters numerous times over the past couple years and could hardly wait to visit their farm—I was salivating in anticipation.

Joining us for this trip was Lane Zirlott. His parents, Brent and Rosa Zirlott, were encouraged to enroll in an oyster farming program offered by Auburn University and instructed by who else but Bill Walton. Brent and Rosa's friend and neighbor, Steve Crockett, was the source of this encouragement. Steve is the owner of Point aux Pins Oyster Company, the first company to join the alternative oyster-growing scene back in 2009 at Sandy Bay in Irvington, Alabama.

The Zirlott family had already made their living on those waters as shrimpers for five generations. Lane is a salty dog at heart: young, married, and strong. He felt that taking the course would be a great fit for him and his young family. Rather than spend more time shrimping on the boat, Lane could spend more time closer to home. He then became fascinated with the idea of growing oysters. It appeared to be beneficial to everyone.

Bill Strength and Terry Strickland joined me for the grand tour and tasting. Rain was in the forecast for the entire week, which is not unusual weather for the

Oyster farmer Lane Zirlott on his family-owned oyster farm with his oyster tumbler/sorter (top). Murder Point's buttery-flavored, briny, and sweet oysters are touted as "butter babies" (bottom).

Ominous skies and a killer welcome sign to Murder Point Oyster farm (top). Cage-grown Murder Points have pristine shells due to frequent tumbling that deepens the cup (top right). Adjustable Australian long-line system (bottom right).

Gulf Coast in the summertime. On this windy, cloud-filled afternoon, we parked my car at the Sugar Rush Donut Store. Lane met us there, and then drove us in his Hummer H3 for the eight-mile trek on a wet clay road. It was the last day of May in 2017, one day before hurricane season started. This ominous day seemed perfect for a visit to Murder Point.

Lane pulled up a basket and offered us some premium and small 2-inch diploids. I shucked and slurped them right away. Some were already beginning to spawn, but for the time of year, they were sufficiently meaty. The pastel purple and white shells had a perfect half-pear shape from frequent tumbling (this is a cleaning, refining, and sorting process that requires an investment of expensive machinery and requires additional farmhands to feed it). The oysters were briny and balanced by sweet buttery richness, just as I remembered them. Personal tastes for salt content in an oyster (measured in parts per thousand) run the gamut. Lane prefers about a 14 ppt salinity before harvesting oysters for a Grand Bay umami finish.

CHICKPEA-CRUSTED OYSTERS
with GARAM MASALA AIOLI

—— *4 servings* ——

Garam masala is a dry mixture of aromatic and hot spices originating from India, Southeast Asia, and much of the Far East. I consider it an amazing, yet lesser-used, spice blend that we American cooks typically don't know how to handle. Wet garam masala mixtures will often include pounded ginger, garlic, and chilies. My garam masala aioli takes those same ingredients and adds them to egg yolks and citrus, whisking them together with drizzles of olive oil, creating a thick emulsified sauce. Once you dab it onto crispy oysters, you'll be one of the cooks in our country with some garam masala expertise.

GARAM MASALA AIOLI

¼ teaspoon ground cumin

⅛ teaspoon ground coriander

⅛ teaspoon ground cardamom

⅛ teaspoon ground black pepper

⅛ teaspoon ground allspice

Pinch cayenne pepper

3 egg yolks

1½ teaspoons minced garlic

1½ cups pure olive oil

1 teaspoon grated fresh ginger

1 tablespoon fresh lime juice

Kosher salt

CHICKPEA-CRUSTED OYSTERS

24 Gulf Coast oysters in their shells (see note on page 99) or 2 pints freshly shucked oysters

1 egg, lightly beaten

1½ cups milk

2 cups garbanzo bean flour

1 teaspoon ground smoky paprika

½ teaspoon freshly ground black pepper

1 cup vegetable oil

Kosher salt

FOR GARAM MASALA AIOLI: Mix cumin, coriander, cardamom, black pepper, allspice, and cayenne pepper in a small cup. In a food processor with a knife blade, combine the egg yolks and garlic, and pulse to process. With the machine running, slowly drizzle in oil and add the garam masala spice mixture, ginger, and lime juice. Run machine until all the oil has been used. Aioli mixture should be creamy and thick. Add 1 to 2 tablespoons of water if sauce is thicker than mayonnaise. Taste; adjust seasoning with salt. If using right away, keep at room temperature. If making in advance, place in airtight container in refrigerator.

FOR CHICKPEA-CRUSTED OYSTERS: Strain the oysters and place in a medium bowl. Reserve the liquor in sealable containers or zip top bags, and place in the freezer for future use. Combine the egg and milk together in a mixing bowl and whisk well. Mix the flour, paprika, and black pepper together in a second mixing bowl. Coat the oysters a few at a time in the seasoned flour mixture. Place onto a cookie sheet in a single layer. Repeat until all oysters have been used. Place the oysters into the egg wash a few at a time and submerge to coat. Lastly, place back into the seasoned flour to coat a second time. Lay them on a cookie pan in a single layer, then repeat with the remaining oysters.

TO PAN-FRY: Heat the oil in Dutch oven or a heavy skillet. Allow ¾-inch of shallow frying oil in the pan, and place over medium heat for about 5 minutes. The oil is ready for frying once you add a pinch of flour and it sizzles and turns brown. Add the coated oysters a few at a time and cook for 1 to 2 minutes on each side (depending on their size), until light brown; turn once. Use a slotted spoon to lift the fried oysters from the oil and place onto a paper towel–lined plate to drain. Fry in small batches until all the oysters have been used. Taste one fried oyster and adjust seasoning with salt.

TO SERVE: Arrange the oyster shells on a platter. Place 1 teaspoon of aioli in the center of each shell, and then top with a fried oyster. Repeat until all the shells have been filled. If using fresh shucked oysters in the pint container, use your favorite oyster platter, stack the fried oysters, and serve aioli in a dipping bowl. Serve right away.

MASA-CRUSTED OYSTERS
with **MANGO MOJO**

———— *6 servings* ————

PAN & DEEP FRIED

This oyster preparation fuses bold, smoky jalapeño and habanero flavors from the Southwest along with a classic Cuban sour mojo that is naturally sweetened with ripe mangoes—a perfect balance of sweet and spicy with crispy oysters. This recipe is one of my favorite ways to cook fried oysters with a "New World" touch!

MANGO MOJO

2 ripe mangos, skins and seeds removed

1 tablespoon minced garlic

3 tablespoons fresh lime juice

3 tablespoons fresh orange juice

3 tablespoons sherry vinegar

½ habanero, seeded and minced

¼ cup coarsely chopped cilantro

¼ cup pure olive oil

Kosher salt

Freshly ground black pepper

OYSTERS

24 Gulf Coast oysters in their shells (see note on page 99) or 2 pints freshly shucked oysters

2 egg whites, lightly beaten

1 chipotle (smoked, dried jalapeño), minced

1 tablespoon adobo sauce

1½ cup masa flour

2 teaspoons ground cumin

1 teaspoon kosher salt

1 pound lard

FOR MANGO MOJO: In a food processor with knife blade attached, add mango, garlic, lime juice, orange juice, vinegar, habanero, and cilantro. Set on low speed, slowly drizzle in olive oil, and process until smooth. Taste; adjust seasoning with salt and pepper.

FOR OYSTERS: Strain the oysters and place in a medium bowl. Reserve the liquor in sealable containers or zip top bags, and place in the freezer for future use. Add the egg whites, chipotle, and adobo sauce to the oysters and gently stir to coat evenly. Mix the masa, cumin, and salt in a shallow dish. Coat the oysters a few at a time in the seasoned flour. Place onto a cookie sheet in a single layer. Repeat until all oysters have been used.

TO PAN-FRY: Melt the lard so that there is ¾-inch in the pan for shallow frying; place over medium heat for 3 to 4 minutes. The oil is ready for frying if you add a pinch of masa flour and it sizzles and turns brown. Add the coated oysters a few at a time, being careful not to overcrowd the skillet, and fry for 2 or 3 minutes (depending on their size), until golden brown. Use a slotted spoon to lift the fried oysters from the oil, and place onto a paper towel–lined plate to drain. Fry in small batches until all the oysters have been used.

TO SERVE: Arrange the oyster shells on a platter. Place 1 tablespoon of mojo in the center of each shell, and then top with a fried oyster. Repeat until all the shells have been filled. If using fresh shucked oysters in the pint container, use your favorite oyster platter, stack the fried oysters, and serve mango mojo in a small bowl along with a spoon. Serve right away.

OYSTER HUSHPUPPIES

—— 4 servings ——

I have deliberately avoided oyster fritter recipes, since they always call for minced or chopped oysters—something of which I am not a fan, unless you're making the silky oyster mayonnaise recipe created by chef Ryan Prewitt of Peche Seafood Grill in New Orleans. There is always an exception! I'm particularly fond of this hushpuppy recipe I created, which of course has bacon, and I adapted one step further—with freshly shucked Gulf Coast oysters. You will need a 1-ounce scoop with a thumb release (a.k.a. disher) for making these perfect gems. Once they float and turn golden brown, break them open—you will find perfectly cooked oysters.

BATTER

6 slices smoked bacon

1 cup yellow cornmeal

¾ cup corn flour

½ cup all-purpose flour

4 teaspoons granulated sugar

1 teaspoon double-acting baking powder

1 teaspoon baking soda

¼ teaspoon kosher salt

Pinch cayenne pepper

1 large egg, lightly beaten

1 cup buttermilk

2 teaspoons strained bacon fat

½ cup small-chopped yellow onion

2 tablespoons finely chopped red bell pepper

1 teaspoon finely minced jalapeño pepper

OYSTERS

1 pint freshly shucked Gulf Coast oysters

3 cups vegetable or peanut oil

FOR BATTER: Cook the bacon in a skillet over medium heat until crispy, remove from fat, reserve fat, and let bacon drain on a paper towel–lined plate. Once the bacon has cooled, chop fine and set aside. Mix cornmeal, corn flour, all-purpose flour, sugar, baking powder, baking soda, salt, and cayenne pepper in a medium mixing bowl. Make a well in the center; add egg, buttermilk, bacon fat, onions, red bell pepper, jalapeño, and chopped bacon. Stir the stiff batter with a wooden spoon. Let batter rest in refrigerator for 1 hour. Meanwhile, strain the oysters and reserve the liquor in a sealable container or zip top bag in the freezer for future use. Lay the oysters flat on a cookie pan not touching each other, and then place in the freezer until firm, about 30 minutes.

TO ASSEMBLE: Add oil to a medium Dutch oven or heavy skillet so it is 3 inches deep. Heat until a clip-on thermometer shows 350°F. Using a 1-ounce scoop to portion batter, fill the disher three-quarters full with batter. Cut each oyster in half and insert a firm oyster in the middle of the scooped batter. Form more batter over the oyster to cover completely and round off with your hand.

TO FRY: Carefully release each hushpuppy into the hot oil, one at a time. Batter should easily fall from the scoop. Deep-fry the hushpuppies a few at a time for 3 to 4 minutes, until golden brown. Fry in small batches until finished. Use a slotted spoon to lift the hushpuppies from oil and place onto a paper towel–lined plate to drain. Let rest for 3 minutes before serving. Great with tartar sauce and hot sauce.

SALTINE
CRACKER-CRUSTED OYSTERS
with ROASTED GREEN TOMATO TARTAR SAUCE

6 servings

When it boils down to practicality, crackers are more often than not an oyster's best friend. Even a seasoned raw oyster lover will use them as a vehicle for building a tasty, personal, one-bite masterpiece. For the squeamish or novice oyster consumer, it's an alternative to slurping directly out of the shell. Crackers can be used as a platform for draping a freshly shucked oyster with cocktail sauce, horseradish, or tartar sauce, or they can be crushed into a medium-fine meal for coating. Premium Saltines crackers are my favorite. I like their texture for frying, and I prefer to crush them myself.

ROASTED GREEN TOMATO TARTAR SAUCE

1 medium green tomato

2 teaspoons apple cider vinegar

2 teaspoons small-chopped fresh dill

1 cup mayonnaise

2 tablespoons small-chopped yellow onion

Kosher salt

Cayenne pepper

SALTINE CRACKER–CRUSTED OYSTERS

2 sleeves (100 total) saltine crackers

24 Gulf Coast oysters in their shells (see note on page 99) or 2 pints freshly shucked oysters

1 egg, lightly beaten

1½ cups milk

4 tablespoons hot sauce (Louisiana brand preferred)

3 cups vegetable or peanut oil

FOR ROASTED GREEN TOMATO TARTAR SAUCE: Preheat oven to 325°F. Cut ends off tomato to sit flat. Cut tomato in half. Place tomato halves cut side up on a pie pan or cookie sheet. Add 1 teaspoon of vinegar over each cut tomato surface, and then top with 1 teaspoon of chopped dill. Bake for 1 hour. Let cool completely and then chop the roasted tomato. In a medium bowl, combine chopped tomato, mayonnaise, and onion and blend well. Taste; adjust seasoning with salt and cayenne pepper. Place in refrigerator for 30 minutes before using.

FOR SALTINE CRACKER–CRUSTED OYSTERS: Place crackers in food processor with a knife blade, pulse to make medium-fine crumbs, and then transfer into a medium bowl. Lift the oysters, a few at a time, from their liquor and place into the crumb; give them a first coating. Place on a platter or cookie sheet in a single layer. Combine beaten egg, milk, and hot sauce in a medium bowl. Use a wooden skewer to spear the coated oysters and dip them one at a time into the egg wash, and then back into the cracker crumb for a second coating. Place them back on the platter or cookie sheet in a single layer in the refrigerator until frying.

TO FRY: Preheat the frying oil to 350°F using a deep skillet and a clip-on thermometer. Tap off any excess crumb before frying. Fry the breaded oysters a few at a time, for 2 or 3 minutes (depending on their size), until golden brown. Fry oysters in small batches until finished. Use a slotted spoon to lift the fried oysters from the oil and place onto a paper towel–lined plate to drain.

TO SERVE: Arrange the oyster shells on a platter. Place 1 teaspoon of tartar sauce in the center of each shell, and then top with a fried oyster. Repeat until all the shells have been filled. If not using shells, use your favorite oyster platter, stack the fried oysters, and serve tartar sauce in a dipping bowl. Serve right away.

CHAPTER 6

OYSTERS ON FIRE

OYSTERS ON FIRE

——— Makes about 2 dozen oysters ———

My primal instinct draws me to cooking over fire, and to the oysters of my ancient past. I have become kind of obsessed with this bivalve, as have many of my friends. Oyster purists and enthusiasts alike celebrate the simplicity of savoring cooked oysters in this manner. I often ponder: When and who threw the first oyster into the fire? Thankful, and with a smile on my face, I can honestly say I will never know. This recipe is designed for the hot blooded, and with only a handful of ingredients! Check it and see. Most of the recipes in this chapter are based off this one.

24 tablespoons (3 sticks) unsalted butter

2 tablespoons fresh lemon juice

2 tablespoons finely chopped fresh parsley

2 tablespoons finely chopped cilantro

2 tablespoons minced garlic

4 tablespoons sriracha

3 fresh Thai chilies or 1 habanero pepper, minced

Pinch kosher salt

24 Gulf Coast oysters in their shells, scrubbed and shucked

Cut the butter into 1-inch pieces, place into a small mixing bowl, and put in a warm area (about 80°F) for 30 minutes. In a mixing bowl, combine butter, lemon juice, parsley, cilantro, garlic, sriracha, salt, and chilies. Stir and mash with a fork until well blended. Follow directions for completing compound butter on page 130.

Follow directions for shucking oysters on page 30. Place one slice of butter over each oyster. Follow directions for handling and grilling oysters on page 130.

TIPS FOR GRILLING OYSTERS

Grilling oysters is a surprisingly delicious experience if you haven't tried it yet. These butter-doused, flame-kissed beauties are a real treat. There are a few tips and tricks you'll need in most of the recipes for this chapter.

Compound Butter: Mix the compound butter according to the recipe's directions. Transfer butter mixture to a sheet of parchment paper, deli paper, or plastic wrap, placing on edge closest to you. Fold paper over and roll into a cylinder, twisting the ends in opposite directions to seal. Place in refrigerator to chill solid for a minimum of 2 hours or several days in advance. Unwrap the compound butter and cut into ¼-inch thick slices. Place the slices on a plate and keep chilled.

Handling: Handling the oysters one by one over an open fire can be trying. It's optional, but in large quantities I suggest using a stainless-steel wire grilling basket or a 10 by 18-inch footed wire cooling rack (available at any commercial restaurant supply store). To get started, shuck the oysters and position each upright in its shell on the rack. At this point, most recipes call for adding a compound butter slice to each oyster. Preheat gas grill or prepare and light a charcoal grill for medium-high heat. Use metal tongs and a kitchen towel. In one move, transfer the oyster-loaded rack directly to the grill and increase the heat to medium high. Let the oysters cook for 5 to 7 minutes.

Finishing: A spray bottle filled with water is good for taming the flames caused by dripping butter should the flames get too high. Feel free to add a bit of additional compound butter over the oysters as they flame and brown a bit on the edges. Let them cook in their own juices until the edges curl, the butter is bubbly, and the shell edges begin to look slightly charred. Remove oysters from the grill and serve right away.

6

OYSTERS ON FIRE

PENSACOLA BAY OYSTER COMPANY
FLORIDA

Pensacola native Don McMahon is in a league of his own when it comes to insurance, and his appetite for farming oysters is even deeper: twenty thousand leagues, to be exact. As a kid, Don recollects being inspired to "farm the sea" after reading Jules Verne's novel *Twenty Thousand Leagues Under the Sea*. As a teenager, Don spent most of his time on the waterways of Pensacola, so it was only natural for him to transition into studying marine biology (and business) at Florida State University.

Don remembers when Escambia Bay was labeled "environmentally unsuitable" to swim in or fish from, only decades ago. Today is a different story. The bay is once again heathy and full of life. On any given day, you may see schools of dolphin swimming the shorelines, mullet skimming the surface, or fishermen pulling up redfish and speckled trout. In 2016, to further revitalization, the Nature Conservatory finalized The East Bay Oyster Reef Restoration Project. Nearly a dozen oyster reefs were restored in East Bay through recovery funds resulting from the 2010 Deepwater Horizon oil spill. A few good things do come out of tragedies.

Don did his oyster homework and has successfully pioneered Pensacola's first oyster farm. For three years, he researched and experimented with ways to grow oysters. In 2016, he purchased oyster seeds that were bred at Auburn University's Shellfish Lab on Dauphin Island and nursed by his business partner Doug Ankersen of Double D Oyster Company in Alabama— Double D is Belle Fontaine's only commercial nursery, which is located on the banks of Mobile Bay. Don has

Maria's Fresh Seafood Market in Pensacola: the first market to sell farm-raised Pensacola Bay oysters on the Gulf Coast (top). An OYRO (oyster roaster) filled with Pensacola Bay Oysters, a favorite preparation in the Deep South (bottom).

Serving up Magnolia Bluff Oysters on owner Don McMahon's boat (top left) and at Jackson's Steakhouse in Pensacola (top right). Don; his daughter, Jane Lauter; and Bill Walton sizing up the very first harvest (bottom left).

two farm locations: one in Escambia Bay, where he grows Magnolia Bluff Oysters (his floating cages are highly visible from the Scenic Highway), and his second farm in East Bay is at a Garcon Point location. Both sites are leased by the State of Florida.

Don's outfit is the Pensacola Bay Oyster Company. Bill Walton and I joined Don for a visit to his farm to check in on his oysters. His daughter Jane caught up with us at a nearby boat slip and we took a short five-minute ride to the year-old Magnolia Bluff farm. Once we arrived, a couple of younger farmhands opened a bag of oysters so we could grab big handfuls to study. Of course, I shucked a few so I could taste them. They were not quite full-sized yet, but already had a fairly

deep cup. They were meaty, with a gentle brine up front and a delicate, sweet finish. For several months after, I served them at the restaurant and at numerous community events. They are among my top three picks, and, in my opinion, one of the tastiest and most beautiful shelled, off-bottom–farmed oysters from all of the Gulf Coast's growers.

While the Magnolia Bluff site receives its watershed from the Escambia River system, the East Bay site receives its watershed from the Black Water and Yellow Rivers. Magnolia Bluff currently has 350 cages, with a first-time grow of 530,000 seeds. The remote Garcon Point setting currently has 85 cages with 60,000 oysters, and 150 more cages on the way. Don, like many

Workers managing oyster seed bags and floating cages at the Magnolia Bluff location, with a glimpse of their Garcon Point location behind the bridge in the background (left). Freshly harvested and shucked oysters (right top and middle). Oyster boat (bottom).

of the other oyster farmers, needs more seed and anticipates the long-term value of seed production. His expansion plans are to open a Pensacola-based oyster seed hatchery and increase his inventory to 2 million oysters.

As no one could have predicted, in June of 2017 heavy rains destroyed Don's entire crop—a prime example of oyster farmers' vulnerabilities along the Gulf of Mexico. Serious oyster farmers often learn by their mistakes, which translates as the hard way. Today, Don is even more determined to come back stronger than before. He has re-seeded for 2018 and even began a small hatchery in Pensacola. I may be Don McMahon's biggest fan!

CHARGRILLED OYSTERS
with **FRESH HERB SHALLOT BUTTER**

——— Makes about 1 dozen oysters ———

One of my favorite ways to savor large oysters—the 3 to 5-inch big-bellied ones with deep cups and big adductor muscles—is to grill them. Also known as "aristocrat" oysters, they are ideal canvases for a seemingly endless array of simple, tasty, yet elegant recipes. Some cooks use melted margarine, but most purists use melted, unsalted butter, which is then formed into a compound butter or stirred frequently over heat into a yogurtlike consistency. Most of my recipes are for compound butter–style preparations.

24 tablespoons (3 sticks) unsalted butter

2 tablespoons fresh lemon juice

1 tablespoon finely chopped fresh parsley

1 tablespoon finely chopped fresh tarragon

2 tablespoons minced shallot

1 tablespoon minced garlic

Hot sauce

½ teaspoon kosher salt

Freshly ground black pepper

12 Gulf Coast oysters in their shells, scrubbed and shucked

Cut the butter into 1-inch pieces, place into a small mixing bowl, and put in a warm area (about 80°F) for 30 minutes. In a mixing bowl, combine butter, lemon juice, parsley, tarragon, shallot, garlic, hot sauce, salt, and pepper. Stir and mash with a fork until well blended. Follow directions for completing compound butter on page 130.

Follow directions for shucking oysters on page 30. Place one slice of butter over each oyster. Follow directions for handling and grilling oysters on page 130.

CHARGRILLED OYSTERS
with **BILOXI BACON BUTTER**

Makes about 1 dozen oysters

According to the *Encyclopedia of Cajun and Creole Cuisine,* oysters were so abundant and cheap in the 1800s that it was hard to find a city on a coast without an oyster house. They were everywhere, especially up and down the Atlantic seaboard. That is where I was raised, and it was the East Coast seafood houses that I worked in during the 1970s. When I migrated to the Gulf Coast in 1982, I brought some of my mid-Atlantic recipes with me. I'm not quite sure, but I may have been one of the first chefs on the Gulf to prepare oysters Clams Casino–style, which originated in New England. I adapted this recipe to bottom-cultivated large oysters and renamed it after the Gulf's casino capital, Biloxi.

¼ cup finely grated fresh Parmigiano Reggiano

¼ cup fine-processed panko breadcrumbs

6 thick slices smoked bacon

24 tablespoons (3 sticks) unsalted butter

1 tablespoon minced shallot

1 tablespoon minced garlic

3 tablespoons finely chopped green bell peppers

3 tablespoons finely chopped red bell peppers

4 tablespoons dry sherry

3 teaspoons Worcestershire sauce

½ teaspoon crushed red pepper flakes

Hot sauce

1 tablespoon finely chopped green onions

½ teaspoon kosher salt

12 Gulf Coast oysters in their shells, scrubbed and shucked

3 lemons, cut into wedges

Combine the parmesan and panko in a small bowl. Cut the butter into 1-inch pieces, place into a small mixing bowl, and put in a warm area (about 80°F) for 30 minutes. Preheat oven to 350°F. Place the bacon slices on a baking pan on middle oven rack and bake until three-fourths cooked, about 8 to 10 minutes. Remove bacon from pan and chop into matchsticks. Reserve the bacon fat for the butter mixture.

Combine the butter, bacon, cooled bacon fat, shallot, garlic, green and red peppers, sherry, Worcestershire, red pepper flakes, hot sauce, green onion, and salt. Taste; adjust seasoning with salt. Follow directions for completing compound butter on page 130 and shucking oysters on page 30. Add a pinch of parmesan mixture and one slice of Biloxi butter over the top of each oyster. Follow directions for handling and grilling oysters on page 130. Serve with lemon wedges.

CHARGRILLED OYSTERS
with BOUDIN & BOURBON BUTTER

Makes about 1 dozen oysters

Chargrilling oysters with sensible and complementary bold-flavored components, such as a quality boudin, andouille, or chaurice sausage with a good-flavored butter, is not a new trend. Big-bellied, mild-flavored Gulf oysters are the perfect canvas for these flavor-packed ingredients when chargrilled. This is my take on a simple combination that is reminiscent of New Orleans, with a Louisiana-style preparation. It's simple, yet explosive in flavor, and uses a few of my favorite ingredients: spicy small-batch boudin sausage, bourbon, and hot chilies.

24 tablespoons (3 sticks) unsalted butter

20 garlic cloves, coarsely chopped

2 tablespoons freshly squeezed lemon juice

½ teaspoon kosher salt

½ cup good bourbon

12 Gulf Coast oysters in their shells, scrubbed and shucked

½ pound (2 links) cooked hot boudin sausage, casing removed

1 jalapeño, thinly sliced into rings with seeds removed

1 teaspoon finely chopped parsley

2 lemons, cut into wedges

Combine butter, garlic, lemon juice, salt, and bourbon in a small saucepot over medium heat until bubbling, about 15 minutes. Turn off and let stand until needed. Before using strain through cheesecloth or fine strainer to remove dark bits of milk solids. Keep warm until needed.

Follow directions for shucking oysters on page 30. Remove oysters from shells; fill each shell with 1 to 2 full teaspoons of boudin sausage, depending on the size of the shells. Place a raw oyster over each sausage-filled shell and press down gently. Follow directions for handling and grilling oysters on page 130. As the oysters cook, ladle the garlic butter mixture over each stuffed oyster. When oysters are cooked, add a slice of jalapeño on top of each, sprinkle with chopped parsley, and serve immediately with lemon wedges.

CHARGRILLED OYSTERS
with **MUSTARD SEED BUTTER**

——— Makes about 1 dozen oysters ———

Turmeric is considered propitious and holy in India, and has been used as a treatment for a variety of ailments ranging from poor digestion to skin lesions. The deep orange-yellow powder is derived from the turmeric plant's root and is most commonly used in Asian and in Middle Eastern cooking. Also called "poor man's saffron," it is perfectly suited for lending color to food, including mustards and curries. The star of this recipe is the popping beer-infused mustard seed; the unique color makes for an eye-catching and savory-flavored compound butter.

BEER-INFUSED MUSTARD SEEDS

4 tablespoons brown mustard seeds

4 tablespoons yellow (white) mustard seeds

1 teaspoon red pepper flakes

1 12-ounce stout beer

COMPOUND BUTTER

24 tablespoons (3 sticks) unsalted butter

2 teaspoons turmeric powder

2 tablespoons finely chopped fresh cilantro

2 tablespoons fresh lemon juice

½ teaspoon kosher salt

OYSTERS

12 Gulf Coast oysters in their shells, scrubbed and shucked

FOR BEER-INFUSED MUSTARD SEEDS: In a small bowl, combine mustard seeds, red pepper flakes, and beer. Seal bowl tightly with plastic wrap and place in refrigerator overnight.

FOR COMPOUND BUTTER: Cut the butter into 1-inch pieces, place into a small mixing bowl, and put in a warm area (about 80°F) for 30 minutes. Place the mustard seed mixture in a small sauce pot and bring to a boil. Reduce heat and simmer gently for 30 minutes. Remove from heat and let mustard seed mixture cool completely, about 20 minutes. In a small bowl combine butter, 4 tablespoons mustard seed mixture, turmeric, cilantro, lemon juice, and salt. Taste; adjust seasoning with salt. Follow directions for completing compound butter on page 130.

TO PREPARE: Follow directions for shucking oysters on page 30. Place one slice of butter over each oyster. Follow directions for handling and grilling oysters on page 130.

CHARGRILLED OYSTERS
with ROMESCO BUTTER

Makes about 1 dozen oysters

Barbequing and grilling are perhaps the world's most universal cooking methods. In the United States, you could consider them rituals. But you don't usually think of cooking oysters on a grill, unless of course you're from the coast. Come into my backyard for a moment because one of my favorite ways to prepare oysters is to cook them over an open fire. And as always, I love using large, mild-flavored oysters and enhancing them with culturally based compound butter. This recipe's butter features Mediterranean romesco sauce made with nuts, roasted red peppers, and garlic.

16 tablespoons (2 sticks) unsalted butter

1 large roasted red pepper, seeded and halved

1 Roma tomato, cut in half

6 tablespoons extra-virgin olive oil

1 slice country-style bread

2 tablespoons minced garlic

½ cup whole or sliced almonds

2 tablespoons small-chopped fresh flat leaf parsley

3 tablespoons sherry vinegar

1 teaspoon kosher salt

1 teaspoon freshly ground black pepper

2 cups grated Iberico cheese

12 Gulf Coast oysters in their shells, scrubbed and shucked

Cut the butter into 1-inch pieces, place into a medium mixing bowl, and put in a warm area (about 80°F) for 30 minutes. Preheat the broiler. Place the pepper and tomato on a cookie sheet or baking pan face side down, about 1 inch beneath the flame. Broil for 2 to 3 minutes until the skins blacken. Turn them over and repeat for other side. Meanwhile, heat oil in a skillet and fry the bread until golden brown, about 2 minutes each side. Let the pepper, tomato, and bread cool completely.

In a food processor with a knife blade, combine the garlic, almonds, and parsley. Blend for 5 seconds. Add the pepper, tomato, bread, sherry vinegar, salt, and pepper. Blend to make a paste, about 10 additional seconds. Transfer the paste mixture into the butter and blend well. Taste; adjust seasoning with salt. Follow directions for completing compound butter on page 130.

Follow directions for shucking oysters on page 30. Place one slice of butter over each oyster. Follow directions for handling and grilling oysters on page 130. Sprinkle with grated Iberico cheese before serving.

CHARGRILLED OYSTERS

with **SMOKY SPANISH PAPRIKA BUTTER & SERRANO HAM**

—— *Makes about 1 dozen oysters* ——

When colonists from the Old World resettled along our coastlines, they discovered a seemingly endless supply of oysters. As New World inhabitants, they also found new cooking ingredients in the flavor-rich lands of the Atlantic and Gulf Coast states. In the 21st century, innovative cooking techniques have continued as cooks have popularized the art of grilling oysters over an open fire with seasoned butter. For this recipe, I did just that by adding paper-thin slices of salty cured ham and splashing the mild oysters with bold Spanish seasonings. The New World is your oyster!

- ¼ cup finely grated fresh Iberico cheese or Parmigiano Reggiano
- ¼ cup finely processed panko breadcrumbs
- 24 tablespoons (3 sticks) unsalted butter
- 1 tablespoon minced garlic
- 3 tablespoons finely chopped chives
- 3 tablespoons dry sherry
- 1 tablespoon minced jalapeño pepper, ribs and seeds removed
- 2 teaspoons sweet smoky paprika (La Chinata brand preferred)
- ½ teaspoon crushed red pepper flakes
- Pinch kosher salt
- 2 thin slices serrano ham or prosciutto
- 12 Gulf Coast oysters in their shells, scrubbed and shucked
- 2 lemons, cut into wedges

Combine Iberico and panko in a mixing bowl. Cut the butter into 1-inch pieces, place into a second mixing bowl, and put in a warm area (about 80°F) for 30 minutes. Combine the butter, garlic, chives, sherry, jalapeño, paprika, red pepper flakes, and salt. Taste; adjust seasoning with salt. Follow directions for completing compound butter on page 130. Cut each slice of ham in half, then quarter each half into 1-inch pieces.

Follow directions for shucking oysters on page 30. Sprinkle each oyster with a dusting of the cheese mixture to give the butter mixture some texture to adhere to. Next, place a slice of the butter mixture onto each oyster, and then divide the remaining cheese mixture evenly among the oysters. Place one piece of the ham on each oyster. Follow directions for handling and grilling oysters on page 130. Serve with lemon wedges.

Oyster Farm
BON SECOUR FISHERIES
ALABAMA

Bon Secour Fisheries in Bon Secour, Alabama started off as a family-run oyster business in 1896. Chris Nelson, a fifth-generation operator, is well-known throughout the nation and highly respected for his Gulf Coast seafood acumen. He offered up a personal tour of the Fisheries' processing plant to photographer Bill Strength, Terry Strickland, and me. Chris provided many stories on topics from cleaning and packing bottom-cultivated Louisiana oysters to their in-house shrimp-processing methods. They have two active shrimp trawlers and a refrigerated trucking fleet that services the Southeast region with fish, shrimp, oysters, and crabs. Chris's operation has approximately 100 employees.

At Bon Secour Fisheries, employees hand-shuck and grade oysters by size to meet restaurant specifications. They also hand-shuck oysters on the half shell and pack them for the famous Drago restaurants, who popularized the charbroiled oyster nationwide starting in 1993. For a select customer base, Bon Secour will machine-clean and sort oysters in their shells and rubber band them one at a time! Once a case is full, they are trucked by the palette to Gateway America, a food irradiation facility located at the Gulfport-Biloxi International Airport. The oysters are then shipped back to Bon Secour for distribution. Chris Nelson caters to his loyal customer base by maintaining both traditional and new oyster handling practices.

Here's an interesting fact. During the early 1990s, the Apalachicola oyster industry in Florida was already in trouble. So, Chris Nelson decided that he wanted to

Bon Secour Fisheries in Bon Secour, Alabama (top). Freshly shucked wild Louisiana oyster (bottom).

Chris Nelson demonstrates his lip-entry oyster-shucking method (top left); sorting and banding oysters for irradiation (top right); in the oyster walk-in cooler with Chris Nelson at his family-owned and operated Bon Secour Fisheries (bottom).

experiment with alternative oyster-growing methods for Alabama. He called upon UF regional shellfish and aquaculture expert Leslie Sturmer. Together, they applied a Florida clamming belt system (a method developed for growing clams on the seafloor) for growing oysters and called it the oyster belt system. Chris was indeed ahead of his time as an alternative oyster grower for Alabama, after being engaged in farming oysters for nearly 10 years.

In the end, the numbers didn't quite add up for Chris, which caused him to pull out of the oyster-farming business. Nonetheless, Chris Nelson and Bon Secour Fisheries are thrilled to distribute these off-bottom beauties for the many Alabama oyster farmers who are strictly growers. On the day of our visit, he had Mon Louis Oysters from Portersville Bay. However, he works with many farmers, including Navy Cove Oysters (Bon Secour Bay), Point aux Pins Oyster Company (Grand Bay), and Bama Bay Oysters (Mobile Bay) to name a few.

BROILED, ROASTED & STUFFED

DEEP SOUTH BAKED OYSTERS

——— Makes about 1 dozen oysters ———

All along the Gulf of Mexico, oysters are baked in the shell with a variety of favorite regional ingredients and served for any occasion, at any time of the year. This preparation may best be described as "the well-dressed oyster" and is one of my most unforgettable baked oyster recipes. I prepared and assembled this recipe with many of the Florida Panhandle's most soulful ingredients in mind. Many of my friends like to call it the ultimate alternative to the Rockefeller-style baked oyster. There are a few extra steps involved in the process, but they are well worth the effort. You will make your life a lot easier by preparing the first three recipes a day in advance. They will store just fine in tightly sealed containers in the refrigerator. Photo is shown on page 148, bottom left.

HAM HOCK BROTH

1 gallon water

2 smoked ham hocks

2 yellow onions, rough chopped

1 celery rib, rough chopped

1 large carrot, rough chopped

2 tablespoons kosher salt

3 bay leaves

½ teaspoon whole black peppercorns

CORNBREAD

2 cups yellow cornmeal

1 tablespoon baking powder

1 teaspoon salt

2 cups buttermilk

2 tablespoons plus 2 tablespoons pure olive oil or bacon fat

2 eggs, lightly beaten

GREENS

1 bunch fresh collard greens

Kosher salt

Freshly ground black pepper

Sugar

Hot sauce

OYSTERS

24 Gulf Coast oysters in their shells

4-pound box rock salt

REDUCTION

1 tablespoon minced garlic

2 tablespoons minced shallot

1½ ounces brandy or dry sherry

2 cups heavy cream

Kosher salt

Freshly ground black pepper

Hot sauce

FOR HAM HOCK BROTH: Combine all ingredients in a 5-quart stockpot. Bring to a boil and let simmer 2 ½ hours. Use tongs to remove ham hocks from the broth to a serving platter, let cool completely, and then pick meat from the bone. Discard skin and bone. Finely chop the cooked ham hock meat and set aside until needed. Strain the broth, reserving the liquid.

FOR CORNBREAD: Preheat oven to 400°F. In a medium bowl add cornmeal, baking powder, and salt. In a small bowl combine buttermilk, 2 tablespoons of olive oil, and eggs; whisk well. Add the wet ingredients to the dry ingredients and stir briefly to combine.

Heat a 10-inch cast iron skillet over a low flame and add the remaining 2 tablespoons of olive oil or bacon fat. Swirl the skillet around so that the oil completely coats the bottom and sides of the pan. If a cast iron skillet is not available, oil a square 8 x 8 x 2-inch glass baking dish. Pour in the cornbread batter. Bake for 30 minutes or until a toothpick inserted into the middle comes out clean and the top is golden brown. Remove the cornbread and allow to cool to room temperature.

Crumble cornbread into small pieces onto cookie sheet. Bake in a 350°F oven for 20 to 25 minutes, until golden brown and dried. Allow crumbles to cool; set aside.

FOR GREENS: Bring the ham hock broth back to a boil. To prepare fresh collard greens, lay the greens on a flat work surface, use a utility knife to remove ribs from leaves, and then cut the collards into 1-inch pieces. Store-bought cut collard greens can be substituted for a fresh bunch.

Plunge cut greens into broth; cook 30 to 40 minutes. Taste; adjust seasoning with salt and pepper; if slightly bitter, add pinch of sugar. Add hot sauce to liking. Strain into colander, reserving pot liquor. Spread cooked collards on baking pan to cool slightly, then chop small enough to fit in an oyster shell; set aside until needed.

FOR OYSTERS: Shuck oysters from their shells directly into a small bowl with their liquor. Discard the top flat oyster shell. Reserve bottom cupped half, and place facing up on a baking pan lined with rock salt.

FOR REDUCTION: Place saucepot over medium-high heat. Add chopped ham hock meat, garlic, shallot, and brandy or sherry. Cook over medium-high heat for 2 minutes, stirring frequently to concentrate flavors and burn off alcohol. Add cream and a few tablespoons of oyster liquor and collard green pot liquor. Stir to blend well. Stirring frequently, let simmer over medium heat until slightly thickened, about 15 minutes. Taste; adjust seasoning with salt, pepper, and hot sauce.

TO ASSEMBLE: Preheat oven to 350°F. Fill each oyster shell with a full tablespoon of chopped collards. Place a shucked oyster over the collards, and top each with generous pinches of cornbread crumbs. Just before serving, place the oyster pan in the oven and bake for 8 minutes. Remove and then sauce each individual oyster with 1 to 2 tablespoons of the ham hock–cream reduction, then place pan back in oven and bake another 4 minutes. Remove and serve immediately.

OYSTER & CHORIZO
CORNBREAD DRESSING

Makes a 9 x 12 x 2-inch casserole

I love spicy ground chorizo, especially in a dressing! Flavors run wild in a well-seasoned chorizo. The bread in the dressing doubles as a sponge, sopping up every morsel of flavor. This recipe is atypical of the familiar New Orleans French bread–style oyster dressing. It's my own Southern and Spanish-inspired conception, and I'm certain you will enjoy it as I have through the years. On a final note, since I'm not a fan of dry dressing, I use lots of oysters and saturate the dressing with extra oyster liquor.

- 2 tablespoons vegetable oil
- 1 cornbread recipe (see Deep South Baked Oysters on page 150)
- 1 pint freshly shucked Gulf Coast oysters, ½ cup plus ½ cup liquor reserved
- 12 ounces ground chorizo sausage (see notes)
- 1 cup small-chopped yellow onion
- 1 cup small-chopped green onion

- ½ cup small-chopped green pepper
- 1 cup small-chopped celery rib
- 2 tablespoons minced garlic
- 3 tablespoons small-chopped flat leaf parsley
- ½ teaspoon fresh thyme leaves
- 2 large eggs, lightly beaten
- 1 teaspoon kosher salt
- ½ teaspoon freshly ground black pepper

Preheat oven to 350°F. Coat a 9 x 12 x 2-inch casserole dish with the oil. Break up cornbread into small pieces and place in a food processor with a cutting blade; grind fine. Transfer cornbread crumbs to a large bowl.

Strain the oysters and reserve the liquor. Place a large heavy-bottomed skillet over medium-high heat, add the ground sausage, and break up to cook, about 5 minutes. Add onion, green onion, green pepper, celery, garlic, parsley, and thyme; cook for 3 to 5 minutes, or until vegetables are tender. Add the oysters and ½ cup oyster liquor, stir to blend, and cook until oysters are firm and edges curl, about 3 to 5 minutes. Empty the contents of the skillet into an extra-large bowl for tossing. Add cornbread crumbs.

In a medium bowl combine the eggs, ½ cup oyster liquor, salt, and pepper. Whisk well. Pour the egg mixture over the cornbread mixture and gently combine with your hands; form into the casserole dish. Cover with foil and place in refrigerator. I like baking the dressing just before serving the meal (the oysters remain plump and are best served that way). Just before serving, bake covered for 35 minutes. Uncover and serve right away. For crispy edges and top, brush on melted butter and place under the broiler just before serving.

Notes: If you can't find ground chorizo, remove the casing from link chorizo and place in the food processor; pulse to grind fine.

   For extra-moist dressing, pour any remaining oyster liquor into a small saucepot. Bring to a boil and spoon over dressing just before serving.

FILTHY-RICH
OYSTERS ROCKEFELLER

—— *Makes 3 dozen oysters* ——

Oysters Rockefeller was created in 1899 at the historic Antoine's Restaurant in New Orleans. It is a culinary tradition all over the Southeast and Deep South, and is recognized around the world. There are way too many legends about Oysters Rockefeller out there for anyone to dare say what recipe is the real one. I was first taught this preparation in 1983 at Les Saisons in Destin, where I was trained by French chef Jean LaFont. Chef Jean prepared a decadent, savory, layered glaze, also called glacage, by combining white wine sauce, hollandaise, and whipped heavy cream. The mixture was then spooned over each oyster, sprinkled with parmesan, and placed under the broiler until golden brown. The title says it all: Filthy Rich!

HOLLANDAISE SAUCE

24 tablespoons (3 sticks) unsalted butter

1 tablespoon tepid water

3 egg yolks

3 teaspoons fresh lemon juice

Pinch cayenne pepper

WHITE WINE SAUCE

4-pound box rock salt

36 Gulf Coast oysters in their shells

4 tablespoons (½ stick) unsalted butter, room temperature

4 tablespoons all-purpose flour

2 shallots, coarsely chopped

2 cups white wine

6 button mushrooms, quartered

½ cup oyster liquor (see note)

1 cup heavy cream

Kosher salt

Freshly ground black pepper

WHIPPED CREAM

1 cup heavy cream

SPINACH MIXTURE

4 tablespoons (½ stick) unsalted butter

2 tablespoons minced shallot

1 tablespoon minced garlic

1 teaspoon anchovy paste

1 pound fresh spinach, rinsed and stems removed

1 cup finely chopped flat leaf parsley leaves

Pinch kosher salt

¼ cup absinthe or anise-flavored liqueur, such as Pernod or Herbsaint

1½ cups heavy cream

Cayenne pepper

Kosher salt

1 cup grated aged Parmigiano Reggiano

FOR HOLLANDAISE SAUCE: First, make clarified butter. Place butter in a heavy-duty saucepan over low heat. Let butter melt completely, about 8 to 10 minutes. Remove pot from heat and let sit for 10 minutes, and then skim off all the foam with a spoon. Line a fine-mesh strainer with a few layers of cheesecloth over another metal container or heavy-duty glass bowl. Carefully pour the warm butter through the cheesecloth-lined strainer into the container. Discard any white milk solids remaining in the bottom of the pan. Set clarified butter aside until needed.

Now, begin the hollandaise. Add water to a double boiler base and place over medium-high heat. Bring water to a boil and reduce temperature to a simmer. Add egg yolks to tepid water in the double boiler bowl. Use a balloon whisk and briskly whisk egg yolk mixture over low heat about 5 to 7 minutes, until ribbon stage—when you lift the whisk, the drizzling batter should form a ribbonlike pattern on the surface of the mixture that sinks back into the mixture after a few seconds. Slowly drizzle in the clarified butter while whisking. Add lemon juice and season with cayenne pepper. Add a few drops of water if sauce is too thick. Remove top bowl and turn off double boiler. Let it cool down for 5 minutes. Hold the prepared sauce in a warm area of the kitchen, or place back into double boiler until needed.

FOR WHITE WINE SAUCE: Place butter and flour into a small bowl and blend together with a fork, until all the flour has disappeared. This is called *beurre manié,* a fancy French term for uncooked flour and butter. Set aside until needed.

Divide rock salt among baking pans; set aside. Shuck oysters from their shells directly into a small bowl with their liquor. Discard the top flat oyster shells. Reserve bottom cupped halves, and place facing up on one of the baking pans lined with rock salt.

Meanwhile, add shallots, wine, mushrooms, and oyster liquor to a medium saucepot. Place over medium-high heat and bring to a boil. Reduce heat to medium-low and let simmer for 15 to 20 minutes or until liquid has reduced by one-third. Add the heavy cream and increase heat to medium-high to return to a boil. Reduce heat to medium-low and simmer until slightly thickened, about 3 minutes. Taste; adjust seasoning with salt and pepper.

Whisk in the beurre manié by pieces until the mixture has thickened. Simmer on low heat for 15 minutes, and then strain through a fine strainer. Set aside until needed.

FOR WHIPPED CREAM: Use a balloon whisk and briskly whip the whipping cream until it begins to thicken like light whipped cream. Do not over-whip. Set aside until needed.

FOR SPINACH MIXTURE: Preheat oven to 375°F, and broiler to medium-high. Melt butter in a large heavy skillet over medium-low heat. Add shallot, garlic, and anchovy paste. Stir with a wooden spoon and shake the pan until mixture becomes tender, about 3 minutes. Add the spinach and parsley and wilt completely, stirring for about 3 minutes. Season with the pinch of kosher salt. Transfer to a mesh strainer and let drain into a bowl. Squeeze the mixture well. Hand-chop spinach mixture small.

Using the same skillet, add the anise-flavored liqueur and place over medium heat for 3 minutes. Stir in cream. Increase the heat to medium-high, and add chopped spinach mixture. Bring to a boil, but watch carefully to ensure that the cream mixture does not boil over. Once the mixture has reached a boil, reduce heat to medium and let simmer for 5 to 7 minutes, whisking frequently until mixture becomes a thick consistency. Taste; adjust seasoning with cayenne pepper and salt.

TO ASSEMBLE: First, make the glacage in one bowl. Use a large spoon or rubber spatula to fold together equal parts hollandaise, white wine sauce, and whipped cream until smooth.

Fill each oyster shell with a generous teaspoon of the spinach mixture and an oyster over top. Top each oyster with a generous tablespoon of glacage. Sprinkle parmesan cheese over each. Bake them for 8 to 10 minutes, until oyster edges curl. Place under broiler for 2 to 3 minutes, or until cheese has melted and sauce is a light golden-brown color. Serve right away.

Note: If you don't have enough oyster liquor, add clam juice or water to reach the correct amount.

PHYLLO PEARL PURSE

Makes 6 single cup servings

The iconic "beggar's purse," a sort of drawstring bag made with a crepe and a blanched long chive, debuted at The Quilted Giraffe in New York in the 1980s. In the years that have followed, there have been as many variations on stuffing a purse as there have been chefs who created them. For this open-style purse recipe, I use thin buttered sheets of phyllo and form them in a muffin pan. The pan keeps all the ingredients together and is simple to replicate. I like to use fresh spicy mustard greens harvested from my own garden for unique added flavor and texture. The purse should remain open to let some of the oysters' moisture escape, and at the same time it will keep the phyllo crispy and delicate.

BIENVILLE SAUCE

6 tablespoons (¾ stick) unsalted butter

½ cup small-chopped green onion

½ teaspoon minced garlic

¼ pound button mushrooms, chopped

4 tablespoons all-purpose flour

2 egg yolks

1 cup heavy cream

¼ cup finely chopped fresh parsley

Kosher salt

Freshly ground black pepper

MUSTARD GREENS

1 pound fresh mustard greens, ribs removed

6 thick slices smoked small-batch bacon, cut into small pieces

¼ cup small-chopped yellow onion

PHYLLO PURSE

4 phyllo sheets

4 tablespoons (½ stick) unsalted butter, melted and skimmed

1 pint freshly shucked Gulf Coast oysters with their liquor

Kosher salt

¼ cup grated aged Parmigiano Reggiano

FOR BIENVILLE SAUCE: Melt butter in a medium saucepot over medium heat. Stir in the green onion, garlic, and mushrooms and sauté for 3 to 4 minutes. Sprinkle flour over the mushroom mixture and stir until the flour disappears and the mixture is smooth. Remove from heat to cool slightly. In a small bowl, beat the egg yolks and cream together. Add egg mixture into the mushroom mixture and stir well. Place saucepot back on heat and stir until mixture becomes a thick and creamy sauce, about 2 to 3 minutes. Add parsley, taste, and adjust seasoning with salt and pepper. Turn off heat. Set aside until assembly.

PHYLLO PEARL PURSE

———— continued ————

FOR MUSTARD GREENS: Fill a large pot with salted water and set over high heat. Once boiling, add the mustard greens. Cook until the greens are tender and bright green, about 1 minute. Shock the greens in a large bowl filled with ice water. Chop and set aside. Place a large skillet over medium heat and add the bacon and onion. Stir until aromatic, about 4 minutes; bacon should begin to brown. Add the greens and stir to blend. Set aside until assembly.

FOR PHYLLO PURSE: Preheat oven to 375°F. Carefully remove phyllo from its box and unroll onto a clean work surface. Immediately cover with a damp towel. Keep phyllo covered as you work. Place one sheet of phyllo on the work surface and lightly brush with melted butter; place a second sheet on top, and brush with butter; repeat until all four layers have been used. Brush top surface with butter. Use a pizza cutter to cut layered phyllo into six squares.

Strain the oysters and reserve the liquor for future use. Place a phyllo square over each hole of a six-cup non-stick muffin pan and gently push down into the pan. Place 1 heaping tablespoon of the greens in center of each rectangle. For each purse, add three oysters over top of the greens and season with a pinch of salt. Add 3 tablespoons Bienville sauce over the oysters, and then sprinkle freshly grated parmesan over top of the sauce. Leave a 1-inch ruffled opening. Brush the ruffled top and sides of purses with melted butter. Bake until flaky and golden brown, about 10 to 12 minutes. Let cool slightly. Transfer purses from muffin pan to individual plates or platter. Serve right away.

Oyster Farm
CEDAR KEY SEAFARMS
FLORIDA

In January 2017, I had the pleasure of slurping Pelican Reef Oysters with Heath Davis of Cedar Key Seafarms. He and his brother Mike are fourth generation fishermen, as well as clam and oyster farmers. The Davis family closed their seafood business in tiny Old Florida Town in 1995, just one year after Florida's net fishing ban of 1994. The Davises didn't start using off-bottom baskets until 2012 and have been producing off-bottom–farmed oysters, named after the reef where they are grown, ever since.

In 2016, Hurricane Hermine caused serious losses for the Davises' oyster crop. They lost a huge number of oysters from their baskets due to Hermine's 15-foot storm surge and heavy winds. Nevertheless, the Davises continued to provide a steady supply of oysters for a few places like Steamer's Restaurant in Cedar Key. This waterside restaurant sells about 3,000 Pelican Reef oysters every week. Heath Davis is determined

Shawn Stephenson, co-owner with Jonathan Gill of Southern Cross Sea Farms in Cedar Key, displaying oysters and baskets of clams (top). Cedar Key Seafarms owner Heath Davis and his customized clam boat (bottom).

to re-seed and stay in the marketplace. Cedar Key's ecosystem is as close to perfect as one can get, yet even in these warmer waters, farmers here are in position to produce the country's best oysters. Their clams are already the best in Florida.

Rowan Jacobsen of OysteRater gave Pelican Reef Oysters a four-star rating, claiming, "These will blow the minds of anyone who doesn't think the Gulf Coast makes great oysters. Beautifully shaped and striped shells, plump meats, and all the sweet-corn goodness of a Cape Cod oyster in late fall (yet this was March). The salinity was strong without being harsh, and the flavor was super clean. This, to me, is further evidence that in March and April, when northern oysters can be so skinny, one should look to the Southeast first."

Briny-flavored, translucent oyster meat grown in Cedar Keys' clean water with the famous Gulf Coast sweet finish from Southern Cross Sea Farms.

CEDAR KEY
Clams and Oysters

Florida fishermen from the island community of Cedar Key began experimenting with the cultivation of oysters decades ago. This was right about the time when Apalachicola wild-oyster production was starting its decline. Florida used to be the Wild West of oyster farming, but the gill-net fishing ban of 1994 had a profound effect upon the long-established tradition of wild-oyster farming—oyster commercial output was in jeopardy. The small community began re-training fisherman as quahog clam aquaculture farmers, and Cedar Key became Florida's first success story for farming clams. Southern Cross Sea Farms has been in the clam business for decades. Southern Cross farmers Jonathan Gill and Shawn Stephenson also have 400 floating oyster cages on Dog Island. They are experimenting with growing Sunray Venus clams and Eastern oysters on shellfish harvesting areas and aquaculture lease sites such as Pelican Reef, Gulf Jackson, Corrigan's Reef, and Derricks.

Daniel Solano of Cedar Key Aquaculture Farms is growing 300,000 oysters in 1,200 floating bags! These Cedar Key farmers began growing oysters only 3 to 4 years ago, when oyster farming was still in its infancy. Along the way, many of these farmers have consulted with oyster experts Leslie Sturmer, John Supan, and Bill Walton from Alabama to troubleshoot and better their regional Gulf Coast oyster-growing techniques.

Pelican Reef oysters on the half shell traditional style with cocktail sauce, lemon, and saltine crackers at Steamer's Restaurant in Cedar Key (top). Freshly shucked Pelican Reef oysters (bottom).

SALTINE CRACKER & PARMESAN-CRUSTED
OYSTERS GRATIN

Makes 2 to 4 servings

I first learned how to cook clam and crab dishes at the beach. I soon realized that a sprinkling of parmesan and saltine cracker crumbs (along with a little bacon) makes everything taste like it's home-cooked and served with love. The same concept applies to oysters. Whether under a raw oyster topped with hot sauce or ground up for breading and broiling, crackers are a perfect companion to oysters. This recipe gets a quick flame-kissed broil under medium-high heat, which is rudimentary to perfect bubbling-encrusted oysters. They're ready to serve in just minutes. It's so simple and delicious.

16 tablespoons (2 sticks) unsalted butter

2 tablespoons minced garlic

3 tablespoons fresh lemon juice

¼ teaspoon red pepper flakes

1 pint freshly shucked Gulf Coast oysters with their liquor

1 large egg, lightly beaten

½ cup buttermilk

2 cups finely processed saltine crackers

½ cup finely processed aged Parmigiano Reggiano

1 tablespoon chopped fresh parsley

Preheat oven to 350°F and broiler to medium-high. Place butter in a small saucepot over medium heat with garlic, lemon, and red pepper flakes. Stir to blend well, and then divide the butter mixture equally among four 12-ounch gratin dishes. Strain the oysters and reserve the liquor for future use. In a medium mixing bowl, combine the egg and buttermilk; blend well. In a shallow dish, combine the crackers, parmesan, and parsley. Coat the oysters a few at a time with cracker mixture and lay them in a single layer on a serving platter. Dip the coated oyster in buttermilk mixture a few at a time, and then coat a second time with cracker mixture. Divide the oysters into each gratin dish.

Bake for 7 minutes, and then place under broiler about 5 inches from heat for 2 to 3 minutes or until the butter is bubbly and oysters are lightly browned. Serve right away.

ROASTED OYSTERS
with **SRIRACHA BUTTER**

Makes 3 dozen oysters

There is usually no halfway for the half shell—when it comes to having a penchant for oysters, you either love them, or not. Depending upon your own unique life experience, you already know this. If you have *never* had them, then this cookbook was in part designed to help swing you into the "love them" direction. Same thing applies to anchovies. Folks either dislike them completely, or ask for extra fillets (usually for their Caesar salad). I found that anchovies pair very well with oysters and spicy garlic butter, giving them the extra brininess they need for dressing after roasting. Drizzle or dip them in this butter mixture as you eat them—it's to die for.

24 tablespoons (3 sticks)
    unsalted butter

1 tablespoon minced shallot

2 tablespoons minced garlic

2 tablespoons anchovy paste

2 limes, juiced

2 tablespoons sriracha

½ teaspoon red pepper flakes

Pinch kosher salt

36 premium or wild Gulf Coast
    oysters, scrubbed and rinsed

In a small saucepot, combine butter, shallot, garlic, anchovy paste, lime juice, sriracha, red pepper flakes, and a pinch of salt. Stir together until melted and set aside in a warm area. Prepare a wood-burning oyster roaster with hardwood and burn down to reach an optimum coal to ash ratio, about 1 hour, or prepare a barbeque grill for medium-high heat.

Place oysters directly onto the roaster flat top or over indirect heat on a barbeque grill. Let the oysters cook for 3 to 5 minutes. Cover with water-soaked natural burlap to help steam while roasting (optional). If the shells do not all open, allow 5 minutes cooking time, then begin removing them from the heat. Use a wide metal spatula or metal tongs to remove oysters from the roaster. Place onto a baking pan and begin removing the top flat shells. If the shells have not popped open, use an oyster knife to open and loosen the oyster from the top and bottom adductor muscles on the shell. Place the loosened roasted oysters in their bottom shell on a serving tray, ladle over melted sriracha butter, and serve right away.

176

178

172

CHAPTER 8

OYSTER PAN ROASTS, PASTA & GRITS

OYSTER PASTA

—— *Makes 2 to 4 servings* ——

I typically pick spaghetti, vermicelli, or angel hair pasta noodles for this dish. Just throw the cooked pasta noodles into the sauce and mix to make sure everything is covered. I love letting the pasta soak in the sauce for a few extra minutes before I serve it—it absorbs more of the flavors and becomes creamy.

SAUCE

- 1 pint freshly shucked Gulf Coast oysters, with ½ cup liquor reserved
- ½ cup chardonnay
- 1 tablespoon minced garlic
- ½ teaspoon freshly ground black pepper
- ⅓ cup extra-virgin olive oil
- 4 tablespoons plus 4 tablespoons (1 stick) unsalted butter, chilled and cut into 8 tablespoons

PASTA

- 2 quarts water
- 2 tablespoons kosher salt
- 1 pound dried vermicelli
- 2 cups pasta water

ASSEMBLY

- ¼ pound grated fresh Parmigiano Reggiano
- 1 tablespoon finely chopped flat leaf parsley
- Kosher salt
- Freshly ground black pepper

FOR SAUCE: Strain the oysters and reserve the liquor. Place a large skillet over medium-high heat. Add wine, ½ cup oyster liquor, garlic, and pepper. Simmer for 5 minutes, then turn off. Add olive oil and 4 tablespoons butter.

FOR PASTA: Add the water and salt to a 3-quart soup pot. Cover the pot and bring the water to a rapid boil. Uncover, add the pasta, and cook for about 3 to 5 minutes, or until the pasta becomes tender, but is firm to the bite (a.k.a. *al dente*). Start testing the noodles for doneness by removing a strand after the first 3 minutes. Reserve 2 cups of pasta water.

TO ASSEMBLE: Place the skillet back on heat; add oysters and 2 cups pasta water. Bring broth mixture to a boil, reduce heat to medium, and simmer for 3 minutes, or until the edges of the oysters begin to curl. Transfer the cooked pasta to the skillet and toss to absorb the broth. Add more pasta water for additional broth. Turn off, add remaining butter, parmesan, and parsley, and then stir to coat well. Taste; adjust seasoning with salt and pepper. Transfer the pasta and oysters to a platter, and then arrange oysters on top of pasta. If there's any remaining sauce in skillet, let it reduce until slightly thickened and spoon over the top of each pasta plate. Serve immediately with additional grated parmesan.

OYSTER PAN ROAST
with **MUSHROOMS**

Makes 2 to 4 servings

The bay scallop prefers little to no freshwater inflow and tends to retreat from the interference caused by human civilization to remote areas in search of pristine water quality. There's nowhere more remote than just east of Mexico Beach in Florida's Big Bend for scallops, and nowhere in Florida is more conducive to growing natural-set oysters than Apalachicola Bay. However, any Gulf Coast oyster (or bay scallop) is ideal for this delicious pan roast with your favorite mushrooms.

TOAST

French bread loaf

4 tablespoons (½ stick) unsalted butter

PAN ROAST

24 Gulf Coast oysters

2 teaspoons pure olive oil

1 tablespoon minced shallot

½ cup rinsed and small-chopped leek

2 cups sliced shiitake, cremini, or button mushrooms (or any combination thereof)

½ cup dry sherry

2 cups heavy cream

Kosher salt

Freshly ground black pepper

1 tablespoon small-chopped fresh chives

¼ teaspoon red pepper flakes

FOR TOAST: Slice the bread on a sharp bias lengthwise to make four pieces that are each 1 inch thick and about 6 to 8 inches in length. Spread each piece with butter on the cut side. Griddle the bread in a cast-iron grill pan or other heavy-bottomed pan over medium-low heat until lightly browned. Transfer each piece to a serving plate.

FOR PAN ROAST: Shuck oysters from their shells directly into a small bowl with their liquor. Heat oil in a large skillet over medium heat. Add shallot and leek and cook until vegetables become tender, about 3 minutes. Stir in the mushrooms; cook for 3 minutes or until tender. Add sherry and increase heat to medium high. Simmer another 3 minutes to reduce liquid in pan. Add cream and oyster liquor and then increase heat to a boil. Reduce heat and let simmer until slightly thickened, about 5 to 7 minutes. Just before serving, add oysters and simmer until edges of oysters begin to curl, about 3 to 5 minutes. Taste; adjust seasoning with salt and pepper. Divide baguette toasts in large plates or bowls and ladle oyster mixture over. Sprinkle chives and red pepper flakes over; serve right away.

OYSTER CIOPPINO PAN ROAST

—— Makes 2 to 4 servings ——

The oyster pan roast, whether joined by tomato and fennel for lunch or dinner, or by eggs and bacon for breakfast, satisfies a need for oysters at any time during the day. The pan roast cooking technique itself is not new to oyster preparations, but has seen a bit of a flavorful renaissance recently. I would say that in the long culinary history of traditional stews, they are not to be overlooked. A delicious example for this is my re-invented version of cioppino, featuring Gulf Coast oysters in a quick and easy pan roast.

ANCHOVY BUTTER TOAST

4 tablespoons (½ stick) unsalted butter, softened

1 tablespoon anchovy paste

French bread

OYSTER PAN ROAST

24 Gulf Coast oysters

2 tablespoons extra-virgin olive oil

¾ cup thinly sliced small fennel bulb

¾ cup thinly sliced small yellow onion

1 tablespoon minced garlic

⅛ teaspoon red pepper flakes

1 cup red wine

1 15-ounce can crushed tomatoes

1 bay leaf

1 fresh thyme sprig, plus more for garnish

Kosher salt

Freshly ground black pepper

FOR ANCHOVY BUTTER TOAST: In a small bowl, mash together butter and anchovy paste with a fork. Slice the bread on a sharp bias lengthwise to make four pieces that are each 1 inch thick and about 6 to 8 inches in length. Toast the bread for 8 minutes at 350°F. Transfer each piece to a serving plate and spread with anchovy butter.

FOR OYSTER PAN ROAST: Shuck oysters from their shells directly into a small bowl with their liquor. Heat olive oil in a medium-heavy skillet over medium-high heat. Add fennel, onion, garlic, and red pepper flakes. Cook covered over medium heat, stirring as needed, until vegetables begin to soften, about 4 minutes. Add red wine, crushed tomatoes, bay leaf, and thyme sprig. Stir and simmer gently, uncovered, for 8 to 10 minutes. Just before serving, add oysters with their liquor and simmer until edges of oysters begin to curl, about 2 minutes. Adjust thickness of sauce to your liking with oyster liquor, broth, or water. Taste; adjust seasoning with salt and pepper. Discard bay leaf and thyme stems. Ladle half the oyster mixture onto large plates or soup bowls. Divide anchovy toast on top and spoon over remaining oyster mixture. Garnish each with thyme sprigs and serve right away.

Oyster Farm

CAMINADA BAY OYSTER FARM
LOUISIANA

In 2011, fourth-generation oysterman Jules Melancon teamed up with Jim Gossen, his lifelong friend, Gulf seafood expert, and oyster fanatic, to plan Louisiana's first off-bottom oyster farm in Grand Isle. The oyster seeds were supplied by John Supan, who is an oyster specialist with the Louisiana Sea Grant program. Jules is using approximately 300 custom-made legged cages that sit just inches off the bay floor, and when harvested, are hand-picked. My scheduled visit with Jim and Jules was nearly interrupted by a severe weather system that swept through Grand Isle with hurricane-like winds, leaving the island without power for two days. A formidable circumstance, but not unusual for the small and remote Grand Isle. Luckily, the power came back on in time and we made the trip.

Jim Gossen knows many chefs and seafood suppliers from around the Gulf, including myself. This made the partnership with Jules Melancon a perfect match. Jim hand-picks the restaurants to work with directly and promotes the off-bottom cultivation method, and Jules grows and tends the oysters. Jules also personally delivers his oysters on Mondays to restaurants in New Orleans. Photographer Bill Strength and I have traveled

Caminada Bay oyster farm co-owner Jules Melancon harvesting oysters (left). Hoisting up off-bottom oyster cages (right).

together to all our oyster excursions, and I knew we would make it to the Big Easy to taste Caminada oysters first-hand Tuesday night.

When we arrived in the French Quarter, we made our way to Dickie Brennan's Bourbon Street Oyster Bar. While there, we slurped Caminada's Louisiana cage-grown premium oysters, which were approximately 3-inches plus, wide-styled, medium-cupped, brimming with meat, briny-bellied, and with plenty of sweetness and chew from the large adductor—just like Louisianans like it.

We also dined at Peche Seafood Grill. The Caminada oysters that were being shucked and served at their oyster bar were a slightly smaller 2 ½-inch version, alongside Isle Dauphine oysters (Alabama) and Alligator Harbor oysters (Florida). The chosen oysters were hand-picked to the restaurant's specifications, which has always been a similar, common practice for Louisiana oyster farmers.

Longtime friends Jim Gossen and Jules Melancon at Jim's Grand Isle beach house (top left). Caminada Bay oysters served at Dickie Brennan's Bourbon Street Oyster Bar in New Orleans (top right, center, and bottom).

BIG BEND CLAM & OYSTER PAN ROAST

Makes 2 to 4 servings

Cedar Key is rich in clams, and oysters are always peaking in Florida's Big Bend Coast under the eastern Panhandle. Interestingly, Cedar Key is barrier island–free and is the second largest clam-producing region in the United States. In Apalachicola, Florida's long-time home of the oyster, it is a fact that natural-set oyster numbers have declined during the last several decades, but are still available. On a broader scope, Panacea, Alligator Harbor, and even remote Cedar Key are farming fantastic oysters these days. For this creamy oyster and clam pan roast recipe, which is more stew than roast, I based the creation on the rich history of the region's famous white-style clam chowder and oyster stew.

TOAST

French bread loaf

4 tablespoons (½ stick) unsalted butter

PAN ROAST

24 Gulf Coast oysters

4 slices thick-cut small-batch bacon

24 Cedar Key middle neck clams

½ cup dry white wine

½ cup thinly sliced yellow onion

1 teaspoon minced garlic

2 cups oyster mushrooms, removed from stem

2 cups heavy cream

¼ teaspoon fresh thyme leaves

Kosher salt

Freshly ground black pepper

1 stalk green onion, small chopped

FOR TOAST: Slice the bread on a sharp bias lengthwise to make four pieces that are each 1 inch thick and about 6 to 8 inches in length. Spread each piece with butter. Griddle the bread in a cast-iron grill pan or other heavy-bottomed pan over medium-low heat until lightly browned. Transfer each piece to a serving plate.

FOR PAN ROAST: Shuck oysters from their shells directly into a small bowl with their liquor. Cut the bacon into matchsticks. Heat a medium-heavy skillet over medium-high heat. Add the bacon and stir until bacon browns, about 2 minutes. Add the clams and wine and let simmer, covered, for 2 minutes. Add onion, garlic, and mushrooms and stir mixture for 1 minute. Add heavy cream and thyme; bring to a boil. Just before serving, add oysters with their liquor and simmer until edges of oysters begin to curl, about 2 minutes. Taste; adjust seasoning with salt and pepper. Divide baguette toasts on large plates or bowls and ladle the oyster mixture over. Sprinkle green onion over and serve right away.

BREAKFAST OYSTER PAN ROAST

Makes 2 to 4 servings

An oyster pan roast is a fast-cooking, often stew-like creation, and is a rock-star meal-in-a-bowl. I believe that oysters pair with breakfast perfectly, and this recipe will put the proof in the pan roast. The star of this dish is the briny-flavored, freshly shucked, bottomland oyster. Their brine imparts the necessary saltiness to the stew. I suggest using wonderful, smoky small-batch bacon and farm-fresh eggs for this dish. As always, the fresher the ingredients, the better.

TOAST

French bread loaf

POTATO MIXTURE

8 slices thick-sliced bacon, cut into matchsticks

2 cups medium-diced potato, steamed until tender

½ cup small-chopped yellow onion

OYSTER MIXTURE

24 Gulf Coast oysters

10 ounces fresh spinach, large stems removed

1 cup halved cherry tomatoes

Kosher salt

Freshly ground black pepper

EGGS

¼ cup good olive oil

4 large eggs

FOR TOAST: Slice the bread on a sharp bias lengthwise to make four pieces that are each 1 inch thick and about 6 to 8 inches in length.

FOR POTATO MIXTURE: Place a large skillet over medium-high heat; add the bacon and cook 3 to 4 minutes. As bacon renders, push bacon to one side of the skillet. Soak and toast the French bread slices in bacon fat one or two at a time, then set aside until assembly. Add potato and onion, stir in with bacon, and cook until crispy, about 3 to 4 minutes. Use a slotted spoon to lift the potato mixture onto a paper towel–lined plate to drain.

FOR OYSTER MIXTURE: Shuck oysters from their shells directly into a small bowl with their liquor. Using the same pan, add oysters with their liquor, spinach, and tomatoes; increase heat to medium high, stirring occasionally until spinach wilts, oysters become firm, and tomatoes have warmed, about 3 minutes. Taste the juices; adjust seasoning with salt and pepper. Remove from heat and set aside.

BREAKFAST OYSTER PAN ROAST

—— continued ——

FOR EGGS: Place a large non-stick frying pan on medium-low heat, add olive oil, and heat for 1 minute. Crack the eggs into the pan, leaving 1 inch between each. The amount of oil should cover the surface of the eggs once they are in the pan so they are being poached. Add additional oil if needed. Adjust heat to low; you'll see the whites start to change color. Cook until the tops of the whites are set but the yolk is still runny, about 2 to 3 minutes.

TO ASSEMBLE: Divide toasted French bread onto plates or bowls. Spoon the oyster mixture around toast. Sprinkle potato mixture onto oyster mixture. Dab eggs with a paper towel to remove excess oil. Use a rubber spatula to slide the sunny side-up poached eggs directly over the bread. Freshly grated parmesan over top would be an excellent addition. Serve right away.

SPICY OYSTER PAN ROAST

Makes 2 to 4 servings

Sriracha: I love you, but you're not the only oyster in the stew. You're a favorite of mine, long before they threatened to shut down the manufacturing plant several years back. What I can tell you is, there are many brands of hot chili sauces that could easily be substituted to add heat to a compound butter. That said, sriracha is still the best. I keep sriracha butter in my collection of compound butters in my freezer at home. Here's my simple and quick spicy oyster pan roast, perfect as an appetizer, or simply double it to make an entrée. The best part is sopping up every drop with French bread!

TOAST

French bread loaf

PAN ROAST

24 Gulf Coast oysters

8 tablespoons sriracha compound butter, chilled

(see Oysters on Fire recipe on page 128)

1 jalapeño, seeded and minced

Kosher salt

Freshly ground black pepper

2 tablespoons small-chopped fresh cilantro

FOR TOAST: Slice the bread on a sharp bias lengthwise to make four pieces that are each 1 inch thick and about 6 to 8 inches in length. Preheat oven to 350°F. Toast for 8 to 10 minutes until lightly browned. Transfer each piece to a serving plate until needed.

FOR PAN ROAST: Shuck oysters from their shells directly into a small bowl with their liquor. Heat sriracha butter in a medium-heavy skillet over medium-high heat. Add oysters with their liquor and simmer until edges of oysters begin to curl, about 3 to 5 minutes. Stir in jalapeño. Taste; adjust seasoning with salt and pepper. Divide baguette toasts on large plates or bowls and ladle over oyster mixture. Garnish with chopped cilantro and serve right away.

TRIPLE N OYSTER FARM
LOUISIANA

Just a couple of hours after my one and only opportunity to tour Grand Isle and the Caminada Bay Oyster Farm was initially canceled, I got a message from Steve Polluck of Triple N Oyster Farm. Steve is practically a next-door neighbor to Caminada Bay Oyster Farm and it just so happened that he was already on my list. His farm is in nearby Area 13 of Jefferson Parish. In the email, Steve said, "The power just came back on and it's going to be gorgeous the next couple days." And then in a second email he asked, "You're not coming?!" I rallied, as I am famous for, and off to Grand Isle we drove. It was a semi-short, 5-hour drive to bayou country. As we drove onto Grand Isle, we took note of the power company in their mud boats still reinforcing power poles, and tending to the countless downed power lines and connections.

Steve and his wife, Ginger Brininstool, were kind enough to invite us to stay at their Grand Isle house and later took us out to see their farm. Steve also went out of his way for us by putting off correcting his students' test papers for the upcoming week. What a guy! Both taught biology courses at LSU in Baton Rouge. Ginger conceived the idea for Triple N back in 2014 after she read an article about the Port Commission of Grand Isle leasing plots of water in Caminada Bay for alternative oyster farming.

Steve is a salty dog at heart and savors every moment tending their 300 floating bags in Caminada Bay, where they raise approximately 150,000 oysters from 6mm seeds and can harvest thousands of oysters

Oyster farmer Steve Polluck at his family-owned Triple N Oyster Farm in Caminada Bay (top). Some of Caminada Bay's briniest and fullest-bodied boutique oysters, with that Gulf Coast sweet finish we're so famous for.

in just 10 months on their 2-acre lease. The couple, along with the help of their two children, are the sole operators of Triple N Oyster Farm. When they are not farming, the entire family goes out boating, kayaking, netting shrimp, or fishing for drum, redfish, and speckled trout.

Pollock buys triploid seeds either from the Auburn University Shellfish Laboratory, the Michael C. Voisin Oyster Hatchery at Grand Isle, or occasionally Aqua Green at University of Southern Mississippi. Seeds are difficult to come by, and Steve, like many Gulf oyster farmers, is in the process of building his own nurseries for tending seed and for future expansion. By the time this book is published, Steve will be successfully hatching larvae and producing his own oyster seeds: something new for the oyster farmers in the same bay.

Steve tends his oysters regularly and believes that he should get as much as he can for his oysters by holding out for the $1 oyster. That's exactly what he does with his premium oysters, and has no problem selling them. Steve, like many oyster farmers, deals directly with a couple of hand-picked restaurants. Steve's oysters

Me and Oyster Specialist John Supan handling oyster seedlings at the Michael C. Voisin Oyster Hatchery at Grand Isle, Louisiana (top left and right). Looking onto Caminada Bay from the Michael C. Voisin Oyster Hatchery (bottom right).

usually range in size from about 2 ½ to 3 inches. They are deep-cupped, brimming with meat, briny, and buttery with a clean, sweet finish.

GRITS
with **OYSTER PAN SAUCE & PARMESAN**

——— *Makes 4 to 6 servings* ———

This dish is a wonderful combination of two of my favorites: grits and oysters. You don't have to be from Georgia to enjoy grits, and you don't have to be from the coast to savor oysters. Some folks like sweet yellow corn for their stone-ground grits, while others prefer white corn. Some folks like oysters shucked right from the shell for this dish, while others are just fine with using shucked oysters packed in water from the oyster processor. Don't fret, just enjoy. Fresh ingredients, along with a good Parmigiano Reggiano, makes everything taste great!

GRITS

1 cup stone-ground yellow or white grits

1 cup heavy cream

1 cup milk

2 cups water

2 cups grated white cheddar cheese

1 teaspoon kosher salt

½ teaspoon freshly ground black pepper

PAN ROAST

36 Gulf Coast oysters

1 tablespoon extra-virgin olive oil

2 green onions, small chopped

1 tablespoon minced garlic

1 medium tomato, small chopped

⅛ teaspoon red pepper flakes

1 tablespoon finely chopped fresh parsley

⅛ teaspoon fresh thyme leaves

1 teaspoon lemon juice

8 tablespoons (1 stick) unsalted butter, cold and cut into 5 chunks

Kosher salt

Freshly ground black pepper

Hot sauce

Fresh Parmigiano Reggiano wedge for grating

FOR GRITS: Place grits, heavy cream, milk, and water into the top pan of a 2-quart double boiler. Bring mixture to a boil and reduce heat to a simmer. Cover and cook 45 minutes to 1 hour. Stir frequently using a whisk or heavy-duty wooden spoon to avoid sticking and lumps. When grits are tender, blend in cheese. Taste; adjust seasoning with salt and pepper. Set aside.

FOR PAN ROAST: Shuck oysters from their shells directly into a small bowl with their liquor. Heat olive oil in a medium heavy skillet over medium-high heat. Add green onion, garlic, tomato, red pepper flakes, parsley, thyme, and lemon juice. Cook over medium heat, stirring as needed, until vegetables begin to soften, about 3 minutes. Just before serving, add oysters with their liquor and the butter chunks. Simmer and stir butter sauce until edges of oysters begin to curl, and sauce slightly thickens, about 3 minutes. Adjust thickness of sauce to your liking with oyster liquor, broth, or water. Taste; adjust seasoning with salt, pepper, and hot sauce.

TO SERVE: Divide grits into small bowls. Make a well in the center of each and ladle oyster pan roast into center. Grate fresh parmesan over top and serve right away.

189

192

202

194

NEW CRUSTED CLASSICS

NEW ORLEANS OYSTER PO' BOY

Makes 4 servings

The po' boy is nothing less than a classic with a great story! French bread sandwiches resembling the po' boy have undoubtedly existed for centuries, but they were not called "poor boys." Legend has it that during the 1920s, when a striking worker came into Martin Brothers' Coffee Stand and Restaurant in the French Market in New Orleans, the brothers would say, "Here comes another poor boy!" And that was *before* the Great Depression. Food for thought. Whatever you want to call it, this recipe should have you in the kitchen making your own version.

DILL TARTAR SAUCE

2 cups mayonnaise

⅓ cup small-chopped bread and butter pickles, drained

⅓ cup small-chopped yellow onion

1 tablespoon small-chopped fresh dill

1 small lemon, juiced

PO' BOY

2 loaves New Orleans-style French bread, such as

Leidenheimer brand, cut into 6-inch lengths and lightly toasted

Hot sauce, such as Tabasco

3 large vine-ripe tomatoes, cut into ¼-inch-thick rounds

Kosher salt

Freshly ground black pepper

24 fried Gulf Coast oysters (see Simple Fried Oysters recipe on page 98)

12 Bibb lettuce leaves, rinsed

FOR DILL TARTAR SAUCE: Place ingredients into a mixing bowl and combine. Let sit 30 minutes before using. Store in a tightly sealed container for up to 3 weeks in the refrigerator.

FOR PO' BOY: Cut bread loaves in half lengthwise, with one side remaining hinged. Lay cut bread loaves open side by side. Divide ½ cup of the dill tartar sauce between the loaves; spread. Add dashes of hot sauce. Top each with three tomato slices. Season the tomato slices with kosher salt and pepper. Top each with six fried oysters, and then top with two lettuce leaves. Close the bread loaves. Cut sandwiches and serve right away.

OYSTER, BACON & CARAMELIZED ONION TARTELETTE

Makes 4 servings

I'm reminiscing now, taking that first bite of tarte flambé. It was a Sunday morning in 1986. My girlfriend and I headed out for a short visit with her mom in Fort Walton Beach. As we entered her kitchen, her mother was hunched over the counter, rolling dough as thinly as I had ever seen. I looked over as she topped it with bacon, thinly sliced onions, crème fraîche, cheese, and freshly grated nutmeg. Wow. I knew something very special was going on. And it just so happened that Marlyse was from Alsace in France. Go figure. It took just seconds to slice the piping-hot tart like a pie, fold it like a pizza, and put right into my mouth. Sensational! The only ingredient that would undoubtedly make it even better is oysters. So, here's a similar recipe using Gulf Coast oysters!

ONION-BACON MIXTURE

2 tablespoons unsalted butter

1 medium yellow onion, thinly sliced

¼ cup dry sherry

Kosher salt

Freshly ground black pepper

4 slices thick-sliced bacon

DOUGH

16 Gulf Coast oysters

4 4-ounce balls of bread or pizza dough

Flour, for dusting

½ cup cornmeal or semolina for dusting a pizza peel

ASSEMBLY

12 tablespoons fromage blanc (French-style plain cheese)

6 tablespoons heavy cream

Fresh nutmeg

Small wedge of aged Parmigiano Reggiano

Extra-virgin olive oil

OYSTER, BACON & CARAMELIZED ONION TARTELETTE

continued

FOR ONION-BACON MIXTURE: Melt the butter in a medium skillet over medium heat. Stir in the onions and reduce heat to low. Stir until the onions are very soft and beginning to brown, about 15 to 20 minutes. Add sherry and season lightly with salt and a generous grind of black pepper. Increase the heat to medium high or until the onions are evenly browned and lightly caramelized, about 10 additional minutes. Set aside. Cut the bacon slices into ¼-inch matchsticks and render in a medium skillet. Use a slotted spoon to lift them from the bacon fat and onto a paper towel–lined plate to drain.

FOR DOUGH: Position a pizza stone on a middle oven rack and preheat oven to 450°F. Shuck oysters from their shells directly into a small bowl with their liquor. Place one ball of dough on a flour-dusted work surface. Flatten and roll out to an 8-inch thin circle. Fold over edges, leaving a ½-inch edge all around. Repeat for remaining balls.

I like to partially cook the dough first, because the oysters release water when cooked and will make the dough soggy. Sprinkle a pizza peel with cornmeal and carefully transfer the tarts one at a time to the pizza stone. Poke the dough bottoms with a fork to keep them deflated and then par-bake the dough for 7 minutes to ensure a crispy crust.

TO ASSEMBLE: Remove from oven. In a small bowl, combine fromage blanc and heavy cream and blend well. Add 3 tablespoons of cheese mixture on top of each pre-cooked tart round and smear evenly with the back of a spoon to cover the bottom. Scatter the caramelized onion and cooked bacon mixture over the tarts. Grate fresh nutmeg on the cheese, and then arrange three or four oysters on each. Season with a pinch of salt and grate parmesan over the top. Lightly drizzle olive oil over the dough crust. Sprinkle a pizza peel with cornmeal and carefully transfer the tarts one at a time to the pizza stone. Bake 12 to 15 minutes, and then serve immediately.

FRIED OYSTER BANH MI

Makes 4 servings

Both Gulf Coast and Vietnamese cuisines place a tremendous emphasis on traditional ingredients, color, flavor, texture, and spices. The two styles come together in this sandwich recipe. The practice of using French bread to encrust native Vietnamese ingredients is known as the banh mi sandwich. Usually done with pork or chicken, the banh mi is dressed with cucumber, daikon, and carrot, providing a combination of contrasting color and texture, then adding cilantro to brighten, jalapeño for spice, and garlic-chili mayonnaise to moisten. The sandwich can include a seemingly endless variation of substitutions, which now includes Gulf Coast oysters. I modeled this recipe after sampling the countless sandwiches from our local oriental markets. You won't be disappointed!

- 1 cup matchstick-cut carrot
- 1 cup matchstick-cut white daikon
- 1 medium cucumber, peeled and thinly sliced
- 5 tablespoons seasoned rice wine vinegar
- ¼ teaspoon sesame oil
- 4 10-inch French bread or Vietnamese bread loaves

- 4 tablespoons garlic-chili sauce or ground fresh chili paste
- ⅓ cup mayonnaise
- 24 fried Gulf Coast oysters (see Simple Fried Oysters recipe on page 98)
- 2 jalapeño peppers, sliced into thin wheels
- 16 large sprigs fresh cilantro

In a small bowl, mix the carrots, daikon, and cucumber with the vinegar and oil; stir to pickle. Cut each baguette horizontally in half, leaving it attached at the hinge. Lay the baguettes beside each other on a work surface. In a small mixing bowl, combine the garlic-chili sauce and mayonnaise; blend well. Divide mayonnaise mixture evenly over each bread shell. Drain the pickled vegetables and divide equally onto bread bottom. Fill each bottom with six fried oysters. Scatter the jalapeño and cilantro over top. Fold over hinged bread top and then wrap tightly with foil sandwich wrap and a rubber band. Slice and serve right away.

OYSTER BLT
with SPICY REMOULADE

Makes 4 servings

Chef Emeril Lagasse has been residing along the Gulf Coast for years now. During filming of an *Emeril's Florida* episode, he tasted an oyster BLT prepared by my good friend John Jacob, chef and co-owner of Vintij Wine Boutique in Destin. In the South Walton episode of season 3, Emeril's exact quote is, "It's one of my favorite sandwiches in the world!" After hearing that, I called chef John to see if I could borrow his oyster BLT concept for my up-and-coming new lunch menu. He laughed, then said, "Heck yeah, that's your remoulade recipe on that sandwich anyway." Sharing the love—that's how we roll.

REMOULADE SAUCE

2 cups mayonnaise

1 tablespoon fresh lemon juice

3 tablespoons chopped gherkin pickles

1 tablespoon capers, drained

1 tablespoon small-chopped flat leaf parsley

2 anchovy fillets packed in oil or 1 tablespoon anchovy paste

1 tablespoon dry mustard powder, such as Coleman's

2 tablespoons finely chopped fresh tarragon leaves

¼ teaspoon cayenne pepper

¼ teaspoon smoked paprika

4 dashes hot sauce, such as Tabasco

¼ teaspoon kosher salt

1 teaspoon minced garlic

3 tablespoons chopped green onion

2 hard-boiled eggs, coarsely chopped

1 tablespoon water

SANDWICHES

12 thick-sliced smoked bacon strips (about 1 pound)

8 slices country-style bread, ½-inch-thick

2 large vine-ripe tomatoes, cut into ¼-inch-thick rounds

16 fried Gulf Coast oysters (see Simple Fried Oysters recipe on page 98)

8 hearts of romaine lettuce leaves

Kosher salt

Freshly ground black pepper

FOR REMOULADE SAUCE: Place ingredients in a food processor with a cutting blade. Pulse and puree until smooth. Make a day ahead or let sit 2 hours before using. Store in a tightly sealed container in refrigerator for up to 2 weeks.

FOR SANDWICHES: Cook bacon in a heavy large skillet over medium heat until crisp, about 10 minutes. Transfer to a paper towel–lined plate to drain. Lay four slices of bread side by side. Divide ⅓ cup of the remoulade sauce between each slice; spread. Top each with two tomato slices and season the tomato slices to taste with kosher salt and pepper. Top each with two lettuce leaves, four fried oysters, and three slices of bacon. Place the second bread halves on top. Cut sandwiches and serve right away.

CARPETBAG BURGER

—— Makes 4 servings ——

The American tradition of combining oysters and beef steak was practiced as early as the late 19th century. Thick-cut steaks smothered or stuffed with oysters were typical of many of the recipes found in early American cookbooks. Food historians generally attribute the first printed recipe for carpetbag steak to Louis Diat's 1941 cookbook *Cooking a la Ritz*. At Jackson's, and the other restaurants I've cooked for during the past four decades, I've served fried oysters over a thick steak with a fine blue cheese. Now I'm taking it to the burger. Here is yet another off-the-charts recipe, this time for a burger *stuffed* with oysters and blue cheese.

STUFFING

12 Gulf Coast oysters

6 ounces blue cheese, room temperature

4 tablespoons (½ stick) unsalted butter, room temperature

BURGERS

1 pound ground chuck or sirloin

½ cup small-chopped yellow onion

3 tablespoons Worcestershire sauce

½ teaspoon kosher salt

Freshly ground black pepper

ASSEMBLY

4 cornmeal-dusted kaiser rolls, cut in half

4 Bibb lettuce leaves, rinsed and dried

4 slices vine-ripened tomato

FOR STUFFING: Shuck oysters from their shells directly into a small bowl with their liquor. Place oysters in a small non-stick sauté pan over medium heat for 1 to 2 minutes, or until the edges begin to curl and oyster is firm. Transfer to a small bowl to cool and set aside. In a small bowl, combine softened cheese and butter and blend well with a fork, leaving some chunks of blue cheese. Set aside.

FOR BURGERS: In a large mixing bowl, add ground beef, onion, Worcestershire, salt, and pepper. Blend well, and then divide mixture into eight balls. Form each ball into a flat patty about ½-inch thick and place on a baking pan or flat surface covered with plastic wrap. Place 1 heaping tablespoon of compound butter in the center of four beef patties. Place three poached oysters on top of that. Place another beef patty over each and press the sides to crimp the patties together and keep the butter mixture and oysters in the center of each stuffed burger. Repeat until all patties have been used. Heat a large skillet to medium heat; place the burgers side by side with 1 inch in between, flipping only once, about 6 minutes to cook each side thoroughly, 12 minutes total cooking time.

TO ASSEMBLE: Keep covered for 2 minutes before assembling. Assemble burgers with roll, lettuce, and tomato, and serve right away.

Oyster Farm

WAKULLA ENVIRONMENTAL INSTITUTE

FLORIDA

Panacea is just a short 40 miles east of Apalachicola, and there are some new oyster folks working the waters there in Wakulla's Oyster Bay. One such person is Bob Ballard, the Executive Director for Tallahassee Community College's Wakulla Environmental Institute (Tallahassee Community College) in Crawfordville. The other is Rob Olin, CEO of Panacea Oyster Co-op. Bob and Rob have *big* plans for producing oysters. There are currently 38 1.5-acre leases there, which covers more than 50 acres of Oyster Bay. While most of the growers are WEI (Wakulla Environmental Institute) oyster ranchers, some are independent.

Most of the students from WEI are farming in Oyster Bay and the surrounding areas of Wakulla County.

Oyster Bay in Wakulla County is an estuary blend of the Gulf's saltwater, the flow of the St. Marks River, and the infusion of Wakulla's freshwater springs. Rob Olin says that "as of now, at the end of this class in 2016, there are about 45 people trained by WEI for oyster farming (ranching)." Rob also adds, "We don't call them farmers in Panacea, they're ranchers. We're raising animals, not vegetables." Good point!

Bob Ballard started the program and is the primary reason this program is where it is today. Rob praises Bob as a visionary and credits him with being responsible for the success of the more than 20 active student oyster ranches that are already in place, many of which are producing. The institute's aquaculture

Oyster Bay ranchers giving the oysters a good shake to remove barnacles and oyster shell overgrowth.

Reid Tilley, ranch owner of Oyster Boss in Alligator Harbor, at the helm in Oyster Bay in Panacea (left). Bob Ballard and Rob Olin showing their ranches in Oyster Bay; the ranchers are members of the Panacea Oyster Co-op at Wakulla Environmental Institute (right). Percolating fresh water springs provide a near-perfect blending of fresh and saltwater in Oyster Bay, Panacea (bottom).

program had 25 students on their waiting list as of this writing.

On a particularly gorgeous January morning, freelance photographers Bill Strength from Pensacola and Alicia Osborn of *Tallahassee Magazine*, Nic Christie of Crispy Cinema LLC, and I met Ballard and Olin at WEI. We drove separate cars and caravanned to a remote dirt road just a few blocks away from the historic Spring Creek Restaurant. We loaded onto a skiff at Spring Creek Marina and took a short 10-minute boat excursion to see Bob's parents' ranch. This is the *first* oyster ranch to raise Panacea Pearls in Oyster Bay. As we gathered to the bow of the boat to help distribute our weight to compensate for the exceptionally low winter tide, Rob exuberantly explained his unique vision for the success of the Panacea Co-op and their oysters. After that mental appetizer, we arrived at the Ballard farm, where I shucked a handful of Panacea Pearls right out of the basket to check them out. They were thin-shelled, briny, firm, and clear: a tasteful premium oyster.

The co-op is designed for independent oyster ranchers in Oyster Bay to focus solely on growing and tending to their oysters. Rob Olin also owns four leases and envisions the Panacea Co-op eventually producing tens of millions of oysters per year, while gainfully employing hundreds of people. The co-op

The jagged-edged oyster displays new shell growth and a shallow cup from calmer water and natural tumbling on Oyster Bay in Panacea (left). Deborah Keller, environmentalist and ranch owner, proudly displays her succulent OysterMom oysters on Oyster Bay in Panacea (right).

was already in full swing when wholesale operations began in 2016. "We are looking for customers who are affluent, socially aware, and educated," claims Rob. "We're a team resurrecting the Panacea area as the oyster community it once was."

Before Bob Ballard's ranch and Olin's Panacea Co-op came along, Leo, Ben, and Clay Lovel of Spring Creek Oyster Co. LLC had already pioneered off-bottom oyster farming in Alligator Harbor to supply their Old Florida family-owned Spring Creek Restaurant, and although they are no longer in the oyster-ranching business, the Loveles developed a growing number of interested customers—a great thing for Panacea and Alligator Harbor down the road.

Also from WEI is independent rancher and alumnus Deborah Keller, who mentored an up-and-coming young rancher named Reid Tilley of Oyster Boss, as well as Matt and Jolie Hodges of Wakulla Mystics LLC in Oyster Bay. Deborah Keller and Matt Hodges

are graduates from the very first WEI aquaculture semester. Their separate 1.5-acre leases rest directly next to Bob Ballard's ranch! Deborah has been producing OysterMom Oysters since early 2016, and is a career conservationist dedicated to sustainable oyster aquaculture. She worked non-stop in securing the appropriate permits for the very first oyster WEI class and the many to follow for in-water-column oyster aquaculture leases. Deborah, like Bob Ballard and Matt Hodges, currently uses the Australian adjustable long-line method to raise her 200,000 oysters. However, Deborah is moving away from the long-line method toward floating cages. OysterMom is one of a few growers and wholesale dealers in Tallahassee, and her clientele includes local restaurants, caterers, friends, and family.

OYSTER TOSTADAS

—— Makes about 10 tostadas ——

A taco, which uses either a flour or corn shell, is simply a tortilla wrapped around a filling. Crispy-fried corn tortillas are tortilla chips, and are also known as tostadas. "Tostada" translates to "toasted," and there's nothing quite like a quick-fried homemade tostada, hot off the tortilla press. Usually flat and covered with a layer of black beans or refried beans to act as a foundation, the tostada is a ready platform to build upon with toppings such as, oh, I don't know . . . you guessed it, fried Gulf Coast oysters!

TORTILLAS

1 cup masa harina flour

⅛ teaspoon kosher salt

⅔ cup warm water

Lard or vegetable oil

Kosher salt

Finely ground black pepper

BLACK BEANS

1 pound dried black beans soaked overnight (see note)

2 tablespoons minced garlic

1 tablespoon red pepper flakes

1 tablespoon cumin powder

1 tablespoon smoked paprika

1 teaspoon kosher salt

8 tablespoons lard

3 chipotle peppers in adobo sauce, minced

SALSA

1 cup halved and small-chopped red grape tomatoes

1 cup halved and small-chopped yellow grape tomatoes

¼ cup small-chopped red onion

2 tablespoons extra-virgin olive oil

1 tablespoon fresh lime juice

½ tablespoon seeded and finely chopped jalapeño

¼ teaspoon cumin powder

¼ teaspoon coriander powder

2 tablespoons finely chopped cilantro leaves

Kosher salt

Freshly ground black pepper

ASSEMBLY

20 fried Gulf Coast oysters (see Simple Fried Oysters recipe on page 98)

FOR TORTILLAS: In a medium mixing bowl, combine masa and salt. Make a well in the center and add water. Mix together from center out to the sides with your hands. Let dry masa fall into the water. Continue to mix; the dough will start to become lumpy, then it will begin to form smooth dough. Knead for 1minute. Dough should have a smooth texture. If dough is too wet to handle, dust with more flour. If dough is dry and cracking, add more water. Make 10 1-ounce balls. Use your hands to form the balls into rounds. Cover with plastic and let sit for 1 hour before pressing.

Preheat frying oil to 350°F in a deep skillet with a clip-on thermometer. Use a 6 ½-inch hand tortilla press to form tortillas by placing dough ball between two sheets of wax paper, and then gently pressing. Carefully remove wax paper and slide tortilla into the hot oil. Fry for 2 minutes on each side or until golden brown. Remove tostadas and season with salt and pepper. Place onto a paper towel–lined plate to drain. Repeat until all the tortillas have been fried.

FOR BLACK BEANS: In a 3-quart soup pot, combine soaked beans, garlic, red pepper flakes, cumin, paprika, and salt. Cook over medium heat until beans are tender, about 2 hours. Add in the lard and chipotles and mash some of the beans with the back of a spatula or spoon to make a creamy consistency, while keeping a lot of the beans whole. Simmer uncovered until the beans thicken.

FOR SALSA: Combine tomatoes, onion, olive oil, lime juice, jalapeño, cumin, coriander, cilantro, salt, and pepper in a medium mixing bowl.

TO ASSEMBLE: Place about 2 ounces of cooked black beans on each tostada; use the back of a spoon to spread until about ½ inch from the edges. Place two fried oysters over each tostada and top with salsa.

Note: Place dried black beans in a deep bowl and cover with water, leaving 3 inches of water over the beans. Soak overnight. Strain.

OYSTER LOAF

———— Makes 2 10-inch loaves ————

I was fascinated enough with the "oyster loaf" (an off-shoot of the oyster po' boy) that I followed a thread on social media about where to find a source for one of these delicious culinary inventions near my current home town, Pensacola. Not raised along the Gulf Coast, I started cracking books for more information. I was intrigued to find San Francisco and New Orleans at the center of its disputed origin. I then thumbed through M. F. K. Fisher's *Consider the Oyster,* where she reported *her* search for an oyster loaf recipe. Turns out that Fisher found the oyster loaf in a San Francisco cookbook published in 1935. She liked the way it looked and realized that it was truly the preparation of her dreams, so that's one she chose to share in her book. No matter the source, the oyster loaf is ingenious! I took her cue and lovingly changed it up to the thing that dreams are made of.

CRUST

2 10-inch-wide French loaves, day-old

1 tablespoon unsalted butter, melted

ASSEMBLY

2 cups packed baby arugula

1 medium tomato, chopped

½ cup thinly sliced yellow onion

Extra-virgin olive oil

6 tablespoons dill tartar sauce (see recipe on page 188)

Hot sauce

1 recipe Cornmeal-Coated Oysters with Crispy Bacon (see recipe on page 108)

FOR CRUST: Preheat oven to 350°F. If using long French loaves, cut in half to fill. If using short French loaves, cut off one end. Use your fingers and kitchen tongs to remove the inside bread to hollow out the loaf. Leave a ¼-inch-thick crust. Repeat for other half. Brush the loaves with butter, place on middle oven rack, and toast for 8 minutes, creating a crusty hollow shell. Remove from oven and set aside.

TO ASSEMBLE: Combine the arugula, tomato, and onion in a medium mixing bowl and drizzle with olive oil to coat. Hold the hollowed bread upright to fill. Spoon in tartar sauce and a dash of hot sauce, add a layer of fried oysters and bacon, and then add a helping of arugula mixture. Alternate layering until the crust is full. Wrap tightly in plastic wrap. Repeat for remaining half. Serve right away or keep in refrigerator until serving. Cut loaves in halves or quarters before serving.

OYSTER READING

A Field Guide to Gulf Coast Oysters
The Gulf Oyster Industry Council
Erin Shaw Street and Big Communications, 2016

A Geography of Oysters: The Connoisseur's Guide to Eating Oysters in North America
Rowan Jacobsen
Bloomsbury Publishing, New York, 2007

Consider the Oyster: A Shucker's Field Guide
Patrick McMurray
Thomas Dunne Books; St. Martin Press, New York, 2007

The Essential Oyster: A Salty Appreciation of Taste and Temptation
Rowan Jacobsen
Bloomsbury Publishing, New York, 2016

The Hog Island Oyster Lover's Cookbook: A Guide to Choosing & Savoring Oysters with 40 Recipes
Jairemarie Pomo
Ten Speed Press, Berkeley, 2007

Consider the Oyster
M.F.K Fisher
North Point Press; Farrar, Straus, and Giroux, New York, 1941

Oysters: Recipes that Bring Home a Taste of the Sea
Cynthia Nims
Sasquatch Books, Seattle, 2016

Oysters: A Celebration in the Raw
Jeremy Sewall and Marion Lear Swaybill
Abbeville Press Publishers, New York, 2016

The P&J Oyster Cookbook
Kitt Woohl and Company, Inc. & the Sunseri Family
Pelican Publishing Company, Gretna, 2010

Sex, Death & Oysters: A Half-Shell Lover's World Tour
Robb Walsh
Counterpoint Publishing, Berkeley, 2009

Shucked: Life on a New England Oyster Farm
Erin Byers Murray
St. Martin's Griffin, New York, 2013

The Encyclopedia of Cajun and Creole Cuisine
Chef John D. Folse, CEC, AAC
Chef John Folse and Company, Louisiana, 2012

Foodways, The New Encyclopedia of Southern Culture (Volume 7)
John T. Edge, editor
The University of North Carolina Press, Chapel Hill, 2007

GULF COAST OYSTER RESOURCES

RESOURCES

Alabama Cooperative Extension System
Private Hatchery Development
Auburn University Shellfish Lab
150 Agassiz St.
Dauphin Island, AL 36528
www.aces.edu/agriculture/
aquaculture-seafood

Albert "Rusty" Gaude
Sea Grant Louisiana
Southeast Coastal Advisor-Fisheries
Yenni Building
1221 Elmwood Park Blvd.
Jefferson, LA 70123
aguade@agcenter.lsu.edu

Bob Ballard, Executive Director
Wakulla Environmental Institute
Tallahassee Community College
444 Appleyard Drive
Tallahassee, FL 32304
www.tcc.fl.edu

Bill Walton
Associate Professor (AU SFAAS)
Extension Specialist (ACES)
Oyster Aquaculture Extension
Specialist (MASGC)
Senior Marine Scientist I (DISL)

Chris Blankenship
Director of Marine Resources Division
Alabama Department of Conservation
and Natural Resources
P. O. Box 189
Dauphin Island, AL 36528
chris.blankenship@dcnr.alabama.gov

Chris Nelson
Vice-President Bon Secour Fisheries
17449 County Road 49 South
Bon Secour, AL 36511
cnelson@bonsecourfisheries.com

Dauphin Island Sea Lab
101 Bienville Boulevard
Dauphin Island, AL 36528
www.disl.org

Double Oyster Nursery
Private Hatchery
Mobile Bay
Belle Fontaine, AL
Doug Ankersen
@doubledoysters

Dr. John Scarpa
Associate Professor of Aquaculture
Texas A&M at Corpus Christi
6300 Ocean Drive
Corpus Christi, TX 78412-5800
john.scarpa@tamucc.edu

Jason Rider
Mississippi Department of
Marine Resources
1141 Bayview Avenue
Biloxi, MS 39530
jason.rider@dmr.ms.gov

John Supan, Ph. D.
Research Professor, Oyster Specialist
Director, Sea Grant Oyster Hatchery
227C Sea Grant Bldg.
Louisiana State University
Baton Rouge, LA 70803-7507
jsupan@lsu.edu

Kal Knickerbocker, Director
Florida Department of Agriculture
and Consumer Services
Division of Aquaculture
600 S. Calhoun St., Suite 217
Tallahassee, FL 32399
www.freshfromflorida.com/
aquaculture

Lance Robinson
Coastal Fisheries Regional Director
Texas Department of Parks and
Wildlife Department
4200 Smith School Road
Austin, TX 78744
tpwd.texas.gov/about/administration-
divisions/coastal-fisheries

Leslie Sturmer
Shellfish Aquaculture Specialist
Cedar Key Marine Field Station
PO Box 89
Cedar Key, FL 32625
shellfish.ifas.ufl.edu

**Louisiana Oyster Growers
and Dealers Association**
1339 Carrollton Avenue
Metairie, LA 70005
Ralph V. Pausina
buddypaus@cox.net
John Supan
PO Box 1597
Covington, LA 70434-1597
jsupan@lsu.edu

Oyster South
Coalition for Advancement
of Southern Mariculture
501 (c)(3) non-profit advancing
oyster aquaculture from the
Southern U.S.
Bethany Walton
oystersouth.com

The Walton Lab
Marine Invertebrate Fisheries,
Restoration and Aquaculture
Bill Walton
mifralabgroup.wixsite.com/home

Rusty Grice
Oyster Aquaculture
Business Specialist
Sea Grant Mississippi-Alabama
Sea Grant Consortium
18 N. Royal St.
Mobile, AL 36602
rtg0010@auburn.edu

ALABAMA GROWERS

Bama Bay Oysters
Bama Bay Oyster Farm
Mobile Bay, AL
Grower
Dottie Lawley

Capt'n Zeke's Oysters
Captain Zeke's Bay Oysters
Portersville Bay, AL
Grower
James Morris

Coffee Island Oysters
Consolidated Shellfish
Portersville Bay, AL
Grower
Tyler Kittles

Isle Dauphine Oysters
Mobile Oyster Co.
Mississippi Sound
Dauphine Island, AL
Grower and Wholesaler Dealer
Cullen Duke
Purchase: *www.mobileoysterco.com*

Massacre Island Oyster Ranch
Mississippi Sound
Bridgeview Oyster Company, LLC
P.O. Box 924
Dauphin Island, AL
Grower
Tyler Myers
www.massacreislandoyster.com
Purchase:
massacreislandoysters@gmail.com

Murder Point Oysters
Sandy Bay Oyster Company
Grand Bay
Bayou La Batre, AL
Grower and Wholesale Dealer
Zirlott Family
www.murderpointoysters.com
Purchase:
info@murderpointoysters.com

Mon Louis Oysters
New Oyster Reef Company
Portersville Bay
Coden, AL
Grower
John Webster

Navy Cove Oysters
Navy Cove Oyster Company
Bon Secour Bay
Ft. Morgan, AL
Grower
Chuck Wilson

Old Field Bend Oysters
Coden Beach Oyster Company
Portersville Bay
8370 Hemsey St.
Bayou La Batre, AL
Grower
Mike Bowen

Pass a Huitre Oysters
Anna's Seafood
Portersville Bay
14540 Tabb St
Bayou La Batre, AL
Grower
Ricky Harbison Jr.

Point aux Pins Oysters
Point aux Pins, LLC
Grand Bay
11320 Marine Laboratory Rd.
Bayou La Batre, AL
Grower
Steve Crockett
Purchase: *scrocket@iglou.com*

Southern Pearls
Southern Pearl Oyster Farm
Portersville Bay
Bayou La Batre, AL
Grower
Louis Graham

Turtle Back Oysters
Portersville Bay Oyster Company
Portersville Bay
Coden, AL
Grower and Wholesaler Dealers
Troy and Rebecca Cornelius
Purchase:
portersvillebayoyster@gmail.com

SOUTHEAST SEAFOOD WHOLESALE DEALERS
Gulf Coast growers use some of these locations to sell their oysters. Subject to change.

Southern Seafood Market
1415 Timberlane Road
Tallahassee, FL 32312
www.southernseafoodmarket.com

Steel City Seafood
1301 Pinson Street
Birmingham, AL
Johnny Carradine
steelcityseafood.com

Bon Secour Fisheries
17449 County Road 49 South
Bon Secour, AL
Chris Nelson
www.bonsecourfisheries.com

Crimson Bay Seafood
13100 Wintzell Ave
Bayou La Batre, AL
www.crimsonbayseafood.com

Evans Meats & Seafood
617 21st Avenue West
Birmingham, AL
evansmeats.com/products/seafood

Revere Meats
132 Royal Dr, Forest Park
Atlanta, GA
reveremeatco.com

Inland Seafood Inc.
2527 Perdido St
New Orleans, LA
www.inlandseafood.com

Louisiana Foods
Global Seafood Source
4410 West 12th St.
Houston, TX
Wholesale Dealer
Jim Gossen
louisianafoods.com

ALLIGATOR POINT, FLORIDA GROWERS

Although there are approximately 31 1.496-acre clam and oyster water column leases in Alligator Harbor, I discovered 2 growers producing oysters. Subject to change.

Playing Hooky Enterprise LLC
Crawfordville, FL
Purchase:
playinghookybags@gmail.com
Grower
Sharon Fitzgerald

Bill's Seafood
Carrabelle, FL
Grower
Bill Lartz

CEDAR KEY, FLORIDA GROWERS

Pelican Reef Oysters
Cedar Key Seafarms
Cedar Key, FL
Clams and Oysters
Purchase:
www.cedarkeyseafarms.com
Grower and Wholesale Dealers
Heath and Mike Davis

Cedar Point Oysters
Southern Cross Sea Farms
Cedar Key, FL
Clams and Oysters
Purchase: *www.clambiz.com*
southerncrossclams@gmail.com
Grower and Clam Wholesale Dealers
Jonathan Gill and Shawn Stephenson

Cedar Key Sweets
Cedar Key Aquaculture Farms, Inc.
Cedar Key, FL
Clams and Oysters
Purchase:
custserv@cedarkeyclams.com
Grower and Processor
Daniel Solano

PANACEA, FLORIDA GROWERS

There are approximately 38 1.5-acre oyster and clam water column leases currently in Oyster Bay; I discovered approximately 10 growers currently producing oysters. Subject to change.

OysterMom Oysters
OysterMom LLC
Tallahassee, FL
Purchase: *www.oystermom.com*
Grower and Wholesaler Dealer
Deborah Keller

Southern Oyster Supply
Panacea, Florida
Purchase: *dsassor@gmail.com*
Grower and Equipment Supplier
Denita Sassor

Saucey Lady Oyster Company
Panacea, FL
www.sauceyladyoystercompany.com
Purchase:
tim@sauceyladyoysters.com
Grower and Wholesaler Dealers
Tim Jordan and Walt Dickson

North Florida Gulf Seafoods
Panacea, FL
Purchase: *steve@*
northfloridagulfseafoods.com
Grower, Wholesale Dealer Equipment, and Seed
Steve Cushman

PANACEA OYSTER CO-OP, FLORIDA GROWERS

Apalachee Bay Company
Panacea, FL
Grower
Joel Singletary

Oyster Bay Oyster Company
Oyster Boss
Panacea, FL
Grower
Reid Tilly

Palmetto Island Oyster Company
Panacea, FL
benknightwiggins@gmail.com
Growers
Ben Wiggins and Phillip Bruggner

Panacea Pearls
Crawfordville, FL
Purchase: *www.panaceaoysters.com*
Grower and Wholesale Dealer
Rob Olin

Panacea Oysters, LLC
Boynton Beach, FL
Grower
Jeanne Ray

Oyster Bay Limited, LLC
Boynton Beach, FL
Grower
Anthony Giardino

Wakulla Mystics Oyster Farm
Panacea, FL
Purchase: *hhodges89@gmail.com*
Growers
Matt and Jolie Hodges

PENSACOLA, FLORIDA GROWER

Pensacola Bay Oyster Company
Pensacola, FL
Grower, Wholesale Dealer, and Future Seed Nursery
Don McMahon

LOUISIANA GROWERS

Caminada Bay Oyster Farm
Beauregard Island
Grand Isle, LA
Grower and Wholesaler Dealer
Jules Melancon

Triple N Oyster Farm
Grand Isle, LA
Grower, Wholesaler Dealer, and Seed
Steve Polluck

Southern Bell Oysters
Grand Isle Sea Farms
Grand Isle, LA
Grower and Wholesaler Dealer
Marco Guerrero

FLORIDA OYSTER AND SEAFOOD WHOLESALER DEALERS

Independent growers use many of these locations to sell their oysters. Subject to change.

Barbers Seafood Inc.
510 US Highway 98 East
Eastpoint, FL 32328
stephaniesbarber@yahoo.com
David Barber

Best Seafood Inc.
332 Patton Drive
East Point, FL 32328
howardreeder@yahoo.com
Howard Reeder

Bill's Seafood
406 8th Street West
Carrabelle, FL 32322
Bill Lartz

Boss Oyster Inc.
125 Water Street
Apalachicola, FL 32320
riverinn@gtcom.net
Lawrence Maddren

Buddy Ward and Son's Seafood & Trucking LLC
3022C-30 Highway 98
Apalachicola, FL 32320
13mileseafoodmarket@gmail.com
Buddywardtrking@yahoo.com
Tommy Ward

Coulter Midway Seafood & Market
325 Patton Drive
East Point, FL 32328
Franklin Coulter

East Bay Oyster Company
327 US Hwy 98
East Point, FL 32328
gingercoulter@hotmail.com
Harrison Coulter

Glass Seafood
100 Michael Way
East Point, FL 32328
glass100apalacoysters@gmail.com
John Glass

H. Allen Seafood Inc.
462 Highway 98 West
Apalachicola, FL 32320
Jimmy Allen

Leavins Seafood Inc.
101 Water Street
Apalachicola, FL 32320
lsi@fairpoint.net

Maria's Fresh Seafood Market
621 East Cervantes Street
Pensacola, FL 32501
mariasfreshseafoodmarket.com
Ray Boyer

North Florida Clams
104 Kendrick Road
Carrabelle, FL 32322
Andrew Arnold

Panacea Area Oyster House
12 Jer-Be-Lou Blvd.
Panacea, FL 32346
panacoast01@yahoo.com
Walt Dixon

Panacea Co-op Corp.
Panacea Pearls
102 Ben Willis Road
Crawfordville, FL
www.panaceaoysters.com
Taylor Brook

R.D.'s Seafood
514 Highway 98 East
East Point, FL 32328
Roger Mathis

Two-Mile Seafood
610 West Highway 98
Apalachicola, FL 32320
Stephen Nash

Water Street Seafood
595 West Highway 98
Apalachicola, FL 32320
www.waterstreetseafood.com
Steven C. Rash

Webb's Seafood II
159 Highway 98 East
East Point FL. 32328
webbsseafood@aol.com
Robert Webb

St. Marks Seafood
161 Kinsey Road
Crawfordville, FL 32327
ricktooke@centurylink.net
Phillip Took

St. Teresa Clams LLC.
2350 Sopchopy Highway
Sopchoppy, FL 32358
clayton8@earthlink.net
Clayton Lewis

METRIC CONVERSIONS

In this book, temperatures are listed in Fahrenheit; volumes are given in teaspoons, tablespoons, cups, and occasionally fluid ounces; and weights are given as ounces and pounds. Anything less than one is shown as a fraction. If you wish to convert these to metric, please use the following formulas:

Fractions to Decimals
⅛ = .125
¼ = .25
½ = .5
¾ = .75

Temperature
To convert from Fahrenheit to Celsius, subtract 32, multiply by 5, then divide by 9.

For example, if you wanted to change 350° F to C:
350 – 32 = 318
318 x 5 = 1590
1590 / 9 = 176.66

Volume
Multiply US teaspoons by 4.93 to get milliliters
Multiply US tablespoons by 14.79 to get milliliters
Multiply US cups by 236.59 to get milliliters
Multiply fluid ounces by 29.57 to get milliliters

For example, if you wanted to convert 3 ½ tablespoons to milliliters:
3.5 T x 14.79 ml = 51.76 ml

Weight
Multiply ounces by 28.35 to get grams
Multiply pounds by .45 to get kilograms

For example, if you wanted to convert 5 ounces to grams:
5 oz. x 28.35 g = 141.75 g

And to convert 2 pounds to kilograms:
2 lb. x .45 kg = .9 kg

ABOUT THE AUTHOR

Chef Irv Miller has been working along the Florida Panhandle and writing about the foods of the Gulf Coast for more than three decades. He received national acclaim for pioneering the area's New Florida Cooking during the American Cuisine movement in the late 1980s and 1990s. Miller's longtime commitment has been to sourcing Gulf Coast ingredients and Southern-inspired foods.

In 1999, along with his partners, Chef Miller founded Jackson's in Pensacola. He currently resides as executive chef. Chef Miller is a six-time performing chef for the James Beard Foundation, and is also noted for cooking alongside legendary chef Edna Lewis numerous times, which led to his appearance as a guest judge on Bravo's *Top Chef*.

Miller's regional recipes are included in *Lodge Cast Iron Nation*. His first cookbook, *Panhandle to Pan: Recipes and Stories from Florida's New Redneck Rivera,* was published in 2015.

INDEX

INDEX

RECIPE INDEX

Publisher: Paul McGahren

Editorial Director: Matthew Teague

Editor: Kerri Grzybicki

Design: Lindsay Hess

Layout: Jodie Delohery

Photography: Bill Strength

Index: Jay Kreider

Spring House Press
P.O. Box 239
Whites Creek, TN 37189

ISBN: 978-1-940611-76-1 (paperback); 978-1-940611-77-8 (hardback)

Library of Congress Control Number: 2018940924

Printed in China

10 9 8 7 6 5 4 3 2 1

Note: The following list contains names used in *Gulf Coast Oysters* that may be registered with the United States Copyright Office: 13 Mile Brand Seafood Market; *A Geography of Oysters; A Word on Food;* AmeriPure Oyster Co.; Antoine's Restaurant; Auburn University (Shellfish Lab); Bama Bay Oysters; Bill Walton; Bill-E's Small Batch Bacon; Bon Secour Fisheries; Bud and Alley's; Caminada Bay Oyster Farm; Cedar Key Aquaculture Farms; Cedar Key Seafarms; Coleman's; *Consider the Oyster; Cooking a la Ritz;* Culinary Institute of America; Dickie Brennan's Bourbon Street Oyster Bar; Double D Oyster Company; Drago; Edna Lewis; *Emeril's Florida;* Emeril Lagasse; *Encyclopedia of Cajun and Creole Cuisine;* Florida Scallop & Music Festival; Florida State University; Glenda and Jerald Horst; Granny Smith; Green Knight; Hangout Oyster Cook-Off; Herbsaint; Historic Pensacola Village; Hummer; Jackson's Steakhouse; James Beard; Jim Gossen; Jitney Jungle; John Folse; John Jacob; Kirby; La Chinata; Leidenheimer; Les Saisons; Louis Diat; Louisiana hot sauce; *Louisiana Kitchen;* Louisiana Sea Grant; Maria's Fresh Seafood Market; Martin Brothers' Coffee Stand and Restaurant; Mason jar; Massacre Island Oyster Ranch; Meyer lemons; Michael C. Voisin Oyster Hatchery; Mobile Oyster Co.; Mon Louis Oysters; Motivatit Seafood; Murder Point Oyster Company; National Basketball Association; National Oceanic and Atmospheric Administration; Navy Cove Oysters; *New Larousse Gastronomic;* Niuhi Dive Charters; Old Bay; Outstanding in the Field; Ouzo; Oyster Boss; Oyster-Obsession.com; *OysteRater;* Oyster Bay Oyster Co.; OysterMom; *Oysters: A Celebration in the Raw;* P&J Oyster Co.; Panacea Oyster Co-op; Panacea Pearls; Paul Prudhomme; Peche Seafood Grill; Pelican Reef Oysters; Pensacola Bay Oyster Company; Pernod; Peychaud's; Playing Hooky; Point aux Pins Oyster Company; Rowan Jacobsen; Ruby Red grapefruit; Saltine Oyster Bar; Saucey Lady Oysters; *Seattle Times; Sex, Death and Oysters;* Southern Cross Sea Farms; Spring Creek Oyster Co. LLC; Spring Creek Restaurant; Steamer's Restaurant; Tallahassee Community College (Wakulla Environmental Institute); *Tallahassee Magazine; The Florida Cookbook;* The Quilted Giraffe; The Roosevelt Hotel; The Sazerac Bar; Tabasco; Triple N Oyster Farm; *Twenty Thousand Leagues Under the Sea;* University of Southern Mississippi (Aqua Green); Vintij Wine Boutique; Wakulla Mystics LLC.

To learn more about Spring House Press books, or to find a retailer near you, email info@springhousepress.com or visit us at www.springhousepress.com.

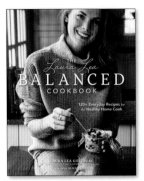

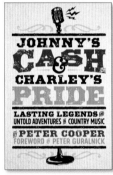
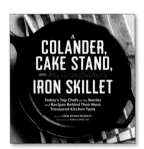

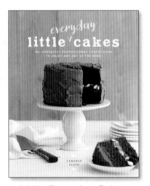